Awakening

To Your

Dreams

by
George DeLong

New World Press

Castro Valley, CA 94546

New World Press
2457 Grove Way, Suite 301
Castro Valley, CA 94546

First edition 1991

Cover illustration:
Michael Drew Designs © 1991 Michael Drew
Concord, CA 94520

Designed and produced by Windsor Associates, San Diego,
CA 92109

Printed in the United States of America

Library of Congress Catalog Card Number: 91-90002
ISBN 0-9628316-0-3

Contents

Acknowledgements

Since the bulk of this work revolves around channeled information, I express my deepest gratitude to the following channels and their "guides": Kathy/Kuthumi, Beth/Siah, Diana/Elija, Mary Ann/Kuthumi and Michelle/Babaji. It is they who made this book possible.

My gratitude to my wife Michelle extends beyond words, not only for serving as a channel and contributing dream material, but for her continuing support and worthwhile comments during a period of almost total neglect on my part.

I am also thankful to my own unseen but not "unfelt" guides who helped me find the words to express my inner feelings, and arrange in order a jumble of transcripts, notes and journals.

My appreciation to Vicki and David, for their valuable comments and ideas, and to Audry for her insightful observations. Michael deserves special recognition for taking my rough sketch and transforming it into a brilliant work of cover art. Also, I am indebted to my many students whose contributions are sprinkled throughout this book.

Finally, I wish to thank those dream researchers whose path I have followed. While we may not necessarily always agree with one another, we share a common goal: to expand our comprehension of a complex multidimensional inner universe, whose workings consist of the very fabric of our being—woven in the breath of our creation.

Preface

My first experience with channeling began during a time spent with Kathy, a charming brunette who I first met when she chose to join our little group. For over a year, I gave classes that focused on spiritual and metaphysical issues, pursuing the goal of self-awareness. All present, our group numbering about ten, met weekly in my home. Kathy was a recent member, having been with us only a couple of months. One day she excitedly phoned me with a very interesting story. While trying to decipher a dream as part of her homework assignment, she began receiving strong psychic impressions, as if someone were telepathically attempting to communicate with her. The "voice" infiltrating her mind was clear and strong, asking her to write down all that was said. Anxiously desiring to share her experience, she called me. Haltingly, she described what happened. Then, as if someone were eavesdropping, her voice dropped to almost a whisper, "I don't know who or what this is," she said, with a hint of alarm in her voice. "I only know it's not me."

My curiosity sufficiently aroused, we arranged to meet at my house the following afternoon. She arrived promptly the next day, armed with a large brown manila envelope. Wasting no time in examining its contents, I carefully began studying the handwritten material. Although appearing to be the work of someone with great spiritual insight, it could also be simply a composition by an alter ego, pilfering data from the subconscious archives of her mind. Not wanting to jump to conclusions, I decided to take a "wait and see" attitude, attempting to maintain an impartial position. The excited quickening of my solar plexus however, belied my attempt at neutrality.

Over a course of several weeks the writings increased, as

did my interest. Kathy would bring the material she "received" to class each week. At first we kept it to ourselves, choosing not to share our experience with the other group members until we felt more comfortable with it. After class, we would pore over the material and exchange opinions. One evening, after reading detailed descriptions of each group member's spiritual development, I could restrain myself no longer. "Is it possible for me to speak with this being?" I asked.

"Just a minute." She replied.

As she lowered her gaze, only her knit brows gave evidence she was relaying my question. I waited in silence. Suddenly, the furrows vanished, replaced by a curious smile.

"He says he thought you would never ask."

Little did I know that from that moment on, my life would take a different turn. Soon I would explore areas I knew existed, but felt were reserved for those of a much higher spiritual caliber than myself. Shortly afterward, Kathy moved in with me. Using various techniques given her by our ethereal friend, she continued opening and strengthening herself as a channel. In the process, she began developing strong clairvoyant abilities.

During this time, I scrutinized every word that came from our invisible companion. Familiar with a psychological condition known as *dissociative reaction* (a multiple personality disorder), I probed Kathy deeply in an attempt to determine if she was dysfunctional in that area. I also tried to ascertain if this was a case of possession by some discarnate entity or worse, the work of the dark forces. Alert for something devious or covert, I found nothing. As a result, all I could do was follow along, determined not to be taken advantage of, or gullibly duped into doing something I would later regret.

Cautiously, we proceeded until Kathy was in constant telepathic communication with one who asked us to call him simply *Guide*, stating he was once our teacher in a distant past life. I later learned it was one of many that Kathy and

I once shared. What we experienced during the year we lived together is another book in itself. There were manifestations, materializations, astral adventures and considerable psychic development for both of us. However, a combination of incidents and issues outside our relationship took their toll. Eventually and regretfully, we decided to go our separate ways, leaving far richer than when we first met. Since that time, my path has brought me to many who were either already channeling, or had a latent talent for it.

My next relationship was with Beth, who had never channeled before, but like Kathy, began soon after we met. It started with a written message. As she was composing a song, her hand began to write seemingly of its own volition, informing her a being on the "other side" wished to communicate with us. Her new guide said she would do better under hypnosis, and as a hypnotherapist, I had no problem bringing her into a moderate trance. Her ability was as a trance channel while Kathy was in direct telepathic communication. At first I thought we were in contact with the same entity as before, but we were quickly informed otherwise. This individual, who Beth eventually was to channel, contributed most of the material included in this book.

As the years passed the spiral took another turn and once again I was alone. Not that I minded it, in fact, it was during periods such as these that I did my most productive work. Later I also began to channel, hold classes and give lectures. In helping others to channel and acquainting myself with those who were already channeling, I was introduced to many entities, all of whom stated their connection with the Great White Brotherhood. Once I asked why people around me sometimes began to channel spontaneously and others with the ability to channel, channeled more clearly. I was told it had to do with my energy field, which acted as some sort of amplifying catalyst.

Through yet another female channel, I became reconnected

with *Guide*, who originally came through Kathy. Most of the channeling sessions occurred on a one-to-one level, with the channeler being either in a meditative or hypnotized state. In working with these beings my trust in them increased. At one point I tried to get them to help me in deciding where to turn, which path to take, or how I could best help in serving. Yet I would always be gently rebuffed and reminded that it was I who must make these decisions. How easy life would be if we allowed someone else to make all our choices and decisions for us, but alas, such is not the case. Were it so, we would be little more than automatons, mindlessly doing the bidding of others, leaving little if any room for our own personal growth.

Over the years my files and notebooks began to swell with a variety of information. Only a small part actually revolved around dreams. It was this portion, however, that served to form the nucleus of this book. I chose dreams because they are the most direct tool available to aid us in our spiritual growth. Hopefully, I will share with future readers the greater portion of all that I learned in other areas.

Rather than using the names of the many different entities who supplied the channeled information quoted, I have chosen simply to print their statements as I received them, without any particular order other than to fit them in where I felt appropriate, and without reference or credit to the particular entity who presented the material. These souls seek no recognition or reward. They are self-fulfilled and self-realized beings who have long since transcended their egos. Serving in a selfless manner, they hope to aid humanity in its growing struggle with itself and contribute freely all the knowledge and wisdom at their disposal.

Introduction

My interest in dreams began early in life, when I first realized some dreams do come true. I can no longer recall my first precognitive dream, only the awe I felt when something that first took place in a dream actually happened. My earliest recollection of such a dream occurred when I was about twelve years old. Many years later, I realized it was actually an out-of-body experience, but I didn't discover this until many years later. When I was eighteen, I dreamt of mopping floors in a restaurant. A short time later I secured a job in a cafeteria. While mopping floors one afternoon, I had a deja vu experience that I immediately connected to my earlier dream. Many of the details were exactly the same, down to the black-and-white checkered floor, but I had never been in that place until after I'd had the dream. Recalling having such dreams before, I wondered if other people had similar dreams and, if so, how was this possible?

I then began my first attempt at research. Unfortunately, I found little help with the psychology of the times. The classes I took were of the traditional Freudian and Behavioral schools, which offered little in the way of explaining my experiences. These schools of thought have contributed immensely to the field of psychology, but by rigidly holding to such narrow concepts they caused me to misinterpret many of my dreams, leaving me more confused than ever. Disillusioned, I set aside my interest in psychology and went in pursuit of more tangible things. Beginning a career as a jeweler and goldsmith, I eventually became a certified gemologist. It was after my experience with Kathy's guide that I decided to join the ministry. Combining the two, I supported myself with one position and enriched myself with the other.

Although in the back of my mind I felt that someday I

would explore dreams again, I didn't realize how many years would pass before this would occur. In fact, I doubt if the spark would have ever been rekindled had it not been for my spiritual teachers. They taught only in accordance with my willingness to learn, never pushing or prompting; yet they were always there to answer my questions, gently steering me back whenever I went off-course. Many times they met my questions with the question "Why?" I knew they were aware of why I wanted to know and can only assume they wanted me to search more deeply into myself and attempt to uncover my underlying motives. The fact that they knew me wasn't enough. I had to know me!

Even at an early age I felt that chance and destiny are but courses we choose to follow by our own free wills. Little did I realize how closely my philosophy paralleled that of metaphysics. When in my search I discovered this fact, my interest knew no bounds. A few short years later my invisible teachers made themselves known to me, and it was during this period that I rediscovered dreams. I realize now, that in conjunction with my other undertakings, the study of dreams has become a lifelong endeavor. It is from this perspective (which is now considerably broader) that I approach the subject.

After sifting through my material, it became clear that of all the tools available to aid in our soul growth and development, none can surpass that of the common dream. There are many excellent psychic readers, channels and spiritual teachers, but nothing you experience will be as accurate and as revealing as your own personal dreams. Dreaming has its own psychic side, and it is an ability we all share. Once understood, dreams can help immensely in shaping our decisions by shedding more light on a given subject or problem. I believe that every major decision is first symbolically portrayed in a dream. If there are to be negative ramifications, then these also will be conveyed to the dreamer.

With this advance knowledge, dreamers can then consciously interpret the message and choose accordingly, thus adding an additional dimension to their lives.

This book incorporates a blend of metaphysical, spiritual and psychological viewpoints directed at those with a general awareness of these fields. We know that Jung was heavily influenced by metaphysical thought, particularly the Eastern variety. I believe he patterned his *Collective Unconscious* after what metaphysics considers to be the *Race Mind*, and the *Anima/Animus* taken from the ancient principles of *Yin and Yang*. I would also like to call attention to Freud's original assumption that most dreams have a sexual basis. According to my guides, had he substituted the word integration (of which sex is a symbol), he would have been entirely correct. They state integration to be the sole motivating force behind dreaming.

I feel this combined work presents a fresh and interesting point of view. In addition to what I just described, we introduce material suggesting that sexual dreams, for the most part, contain non-sexual messages. An attempt is also made to help the dreamer understand the difference between astral projection and an astral dream. Another area describes how anonymous figures in dreams are symbols of yin or yang influence. Wish fulfillment dreams are questioned, and presented in a new light. Also, the dream guides give an interesting explanation for the occurrence of mysterious "shifts" in dreams. Incorporating their messages with my own findings (as well as those of others), I feel I have substantiated to some degree the material presented. Those familiar with dreamwork will find other interesting and perhaps controversial contributions, which to my knowledge have never before seen print.

I was given these teachings on dreams in a twofold manner. First, I submitted a dream to my guides, from whom followed a complete interpretation. This enabled me to trace backward, moving from their interpretation to the symbols used by the dreamer. In other words, I fit the answer to the question, which served as an example of how a dream works. This was indeed an advantage. Second, there were many question-and-answer periods leading to some very informative discourses; most of those concerning dreams are printed in this book. It has never ceased to amaze me how easily and matter-of-factly these beings interpreted the dreams we presented to them. Having weighed their answers I find them to be sound, as do others who submitted their dreams for interpretation. I now leave it up to the reader to decide the validity of this material "we" present.

My approach is not to make an arduous study of the history of dreams nor to probe or challenge the findings of religious and scientific researchers. I merely wish to provide a few answers, along with a streamlined and comprehensive method whereby one may easily examine their own dream material and come to some reasonable conclusion as to the meaning of its contents. In this respect, I present this material to you and sincerely hope it will enrich your life to the same degree it has mine.

1

Dreams:
A Self-Portrait

What is a dream? In the broadest sense, a dream is an extension of life that takes place as we sleep and of which we know little about. In order for dreams to be fully understood life itself must be understood. Edgar Cayce implies that the dream state is a place where "self" meets self.[1] I feel the same holds true in waking life, and believe that people serve as mirrors, reflecting back to us our own qualities, triggering our strengths and weaknesses in every conceivable manner. Why? The answer is so we may better understand ourselves.

Carl Jung felt that in our waking state of consciousness, we understand others only from the point that we understand ourselves. Gestalt therapist Fritz Perls and Jung both agree that on a subjective level all the characters portrayed in a dream are aspects of the dreamer or the dreamer's personality.[2] If the above is true, then it appears that on both an inner and outer level we are continually being confronted with ourselves. Therefore, we may limitedly define a dream as a self-portrayal in symbolic form, as perceived by the subconscious mind and presented back to us while in an unconscious (dream) state.

Our dream messages often reveal the depth of our feelings by monitoring our actions and reactions to events taking place in our daily lives. The dream mind creates a scenario by personifying these thoughts and feelings as dream objects and characters. Constructing a backdrop or setting, it assigns the cast their roles and the drama unfolds. A continuing saga that could be aptly titled "This is Your Life."

Is life truly a drama wherein we set the stage, selecting the roles we are to play, and the dream merely its reflection? The dream guides who present their information here seem to think so. They suggest even further that our purpose in life is to perfect our roles, with dreams representing an essential evaluation of our progress, thus serving to aid us in this ongoing and integrative process.

I have long felt that dreams are one of the most common ways we communicate with our souls, along with other aspects of ourselves. What is the soul? I consider it to be a term synonymous with what we call the higher self or superconscious, in that it is the spiritual essence of our beings. A spark in some and a flame in others, it remains the innate goodness within us all.

Essentially, we are extensions of our soul in physical incarnation upon the earth plane. Our immediate purpose is to end the karma we have created for ourselves without incurring more. This suggests making peace with ourselves and others, and applies on a collective as well as an individual level. As we grow in awareness, we strengthen our line of communication with our souls. Our dreams then become more spiritually potent or profound, and provide us with even greater insight and guidance.

The human mind is similar to both a camera and a projector, using our feelings as a lens through which to focus. These feelings, prompted by our thoughts are ultimately projected outward as a behavioral response, serving to form a statement. Some are healthy and positive, while others are not. Sometimes we "dump" these feelings onto others in a reactive manner, while other times they are a vehicle with which we express our love and admiration. Our dreams often divulge what triggers these feelings and what causes us to behave in the manner we do.

Dreams are meaningful, complex and multileveled states of existence that serve to further our own individual development. They reflect the past, present and to some degree the future. Intangible and yet quite real, they exist in a timeless realm and occupy no measurable space—residing in a dimension of the mind that exists beyond our physical sphere. If this dream world is a part of us, then we too must exist in some fashion in this other world. We extend an invisible but discernible part of ourselves into a place as solid and real as our three-dimensional habitat. Are we truly multidimensional beings? The inner plane teachers state:

"LIFE IN ITS FULLEST SENSE CANNOT BE RESTRICTED TO TIME AND SPACE, REGARDLESS OF THE FACT MANKIND DETERMINES TO EXPERIENCE IT THAT WAY."

SLEEP CYCLES

We begin to dream from the moment of birth, a continuing process that ceases only with death. Dreaming occurs only while we sleep, leading us to perform scientific studies to better understand the nature of sleep. Researchers discovered that as we sleep our brain-wave pattern undergoes cyclic changes.[3] A machine known as an electroencephalograph or EEG machine enables dream laboratories to follow us through each stage of our sleep period.

A complete cycle consists of four stages. At the onset of sleep we enter a descending Stage One, taking on the appearance of what we call the hypnagogic state. Here, we often see vague forms and nameless faces drifting past. Soon, we enter Stage Two where the body becomes even more relaxed. Later, we pass through Stages Three and Four, where we spend approximately twelve percent of our sleep time before ascending back up to Stage One, which completes the final stage of our cycle. Although the exact amount of time spent in each stage varies somewhat, the entire cycle lasts about ninety minutes. When we approach ascending Stage One something different occurs. We experience rapid eye movement or "REM." This phenomena consists of the eyes moving rapidly and synchronously under closed eyelids, as if we were observing something in the same manner we do when we are awake. If we awaken during this REM period, the chances of our recalling our dream would be over eighty percent.

Gradually, we slip out of Stage One and REM sleep, descending into "NREM" sleep where little eye movement occurs. It was at one time believed that dreams occured only during Stage One or REM sleep, but additional studies indicate this is not the case. NREM dreams are more difficult to recall, with only about a seven percent chance of remembering. The dreams themselves are also different from REM dreams in that they are shorter and more abstract. Reports show that subjects awakened from this type of sleep stated they felt more like they were "thinking" than dreaming. On many occasions the dreams appeared more ethereal than their Stage One counterparts, with shadowy figures and unfamiliar or vague scenes. A feeling of disembodiment and disorientation is not uncommon in NREM dreams.

Dream research, expanding considerably in recent years, is now constantly presenting new findings. Because of the difficulty in providing conclusive evidence to the scientific community and the world at large, researchers must make many painstaking and lengthy studies. With each cautious step, these scientists bring us closer to a vast and complex reality. I have no doubt that eventually many of the concepts presented in this book will be borne out, but until such time we have only theory to rely on. The only problem with that is: Which theory do we accept?

THE FUNCTION OF DREAMS

Dreams reflect our deepest thoughts and feelings, emerging from the depths of our unconscious and resting just below the surface of our waking conscious. Their purpose is to inspire certain developmental changes by integrating any conflicts or feelings we have consciously been unable to resolve. This integrative process, measured in terms of growth or maturation, makes for a more balanced, well-rounded individual. We can hasten this developmental process with encouraging results by consciously working with our dreams. Dreamwork offers much in the way of helping us recognize these hidden feelings we have for ourselves and others.

While dreams commonly reveal our doubts, fears, anxieties, guilts and feelings of self-worth, they act in a compensatory manner to relieve the inner stress and pressure caused by our mental attitude. When failing to shift to a more positive perspective we may encounter a disturbing dream pointing this out. Also, when we arrive at the core of these deep-seated issues we often open the door to some very negative dream experiences. Whenever there is a strongly disturbing influence in our lives the compensatory mechanism can be overloaded, prompting the bizarre and fearful dreams we call nightmares. On the positive side, dreams reflect our strengths and virtues, serving to bolster our morale when it is low by showing us the brighter side of things. Often, they reveal hidden talents sometimes symbolized as riches or treasure. Dreams serve many functions. Once, inquiring about the general function of dreams, I received this reply:

THE FUNCTION OF DREAMS HAS TO DO WITH INTEGRATING YOUR INNER EXPERIENCE WITH YOUR OUTER, WHILE IN INCARNATION. THIS IS SIGNIFICANT BECAUSE YOU DON'T DREAM WHEN YOU ARE NOT IN INCARNATION. IF WE TAKE THIS A STEP FURTHER AND SEE THAT DREAMING IS A NECESSARY FUNCTION FOR AN INDIVIDUAL DURING THAT TIME SPENT ON THE PHYSICAL PLANE, WE BEGIN TO SEE THE TRUE FUNCTION OF DREAMING. THAT IS, TO HELP THE INDIVIDUAL ADJUST TO AND WORK THROUGH THE EXPERIENCES AND ISSUES INVOLVED. THIS IS BECAUSE THEY ARE IN A BODY AND TEND TO IDENTIFY WITH THAT BODY MORE SO THAN WITH THE INTANGIBLE QUAL-ITIES OF THE SOUL. THIS CREATES THE DRA-MATIC DUALITY OF A SOUL THAT THINKS IT'S A BODY. WITH THIS TYPE OF CONFLICT IN PROGRESS YOU MUST HAVE A MEDIATOR, AND THAT IS EXACTLY WHAT A DREAM IS.

Life is a series of experiences and expressions and the most common way in which we express ourselves is through our feelings. Unfortunately, we are often in a position where we cannot or will not express these feelings. Sometimes we choose not to acknowledge them at all. When we choose not to acknowledge, evaluate or in some way deal with these feelings on a conscious level, they become relegated to the graveyard of our unconscious where they eventually come back to haunt us. I think of this area as a garbage dump filled with everything we have ever "stuffed." Whenever our outer expression is not in keeping with our inner feelings—we are suppressing. However, as my dream guides succintly stated: **"WHATEVER WE SUPPRESS THE DREAM WILL EXPRESS."**

Suppression can create a conflict within the psyche, resulting in a disturbance or imbalance in need of correction. Dreams allow us to release much of the pressure created from this inner conflict. This is perhaps why we need more sleep when in a depressed or otherwise disturbed state. This processing function constitutes a means of integrating submerged or repressed feelings in a manner that allows us to unconsciously assimilate them to some degree.

THE HEALING FUNCTION OF DREAMS

The healing function of dreams has to do with integrating our inner experience with our outer, helping us to deal with and work through the issues at hand. The hypothesis of Jung is that the psyche has a "self-regulating system" that serves to maintain balance by a process of the unconscious which he calls "compensation and complementation."[4] Compensation adjusts erroneous attitudes by painting a "different" and more complete picture from what we had in mind, while complementation supplies missing details that we consciously omit or repress. If, for example, we repress certain conscious attitudes or feelings, they must appear on an unconscious level. It is much like squeezing a half-filled balloon. The part we squeeze reduces almost to nothing while the other portion expands to twice its original size. In order to reinstitute a balance between the conscious and unconscious, a dream emerges that compensates for what is lacking in the conscious attitude of the dreamer. An example of complementation would be if the conscious attitude of the dreamer is to a certain extent one-sided, and the dream takes the opposite side to complement. This does not necessarily mean taking a stand in opposition to the dreamer's viewpoint, merely a different point of view, usually closer to the truth.

"WHERE ONE'S VISION IS FAULTY THE DREAM WILL CLARIFY." It appears that whenever we omit, resist or distort the truth as it presents itself to us in waking life, we upset a balance that in some way must be corrected. This is exactly what a dream does. Sometimes the degree of forcefulness or exaggeration found in a dream reflects the degree to which the dreamer has upset this balance. We often make the claim that "No one knows us better than ourselves." Yet, how often have we witnessed others who were totally oblivious to their actions? Actually, it is quite easy to cloud an issue purposefully in our minds so as not to see ourselves in a true light. We can mentally rearrange our behavior to make whatever we do appear justifiable, presentable or acceptable, but not so in the dream state. If there is an area within ourselves we fail to see consciously, our dreams will help to shed some light.

Occasionally, within the dream we play out both sides of a relationship, with emphasis on the opposite side, to better understand what the other person is going through. This helps us gain a better and more balanced perspective. In our waking state we usually have to deal with our ego, which tends to downplay or otherwise obscure the truth of the issue. Time and again, I have found our dreams presenting us with a clearer and more truthful perspective of ourselves and our experience. There appears to be a mechanism at work that will not allow us to integrate an experience based upon self-imposed ignorance or deception. On some level we must maintain an impartial view to balance such feelings. We derive maximum conscious benefit from dreamwork by keeping an open and objective mind.

The ultimate goal of dreamwork is to reach a point where we may interpret our dreams through intuition and without a great deal of effort. This can only be accomplished by narrowing the gap between our conscious and unconscious minds. It can be done in part through self-understanding, and in part by the changes we make in light of that self-understanding. The importance of dreamwork is found in allowing the dream a fuller expression in our conscious life.

Only by promoting conscious cooperation between the dream and ourselves can we bring it into fuller manifestation. By viewing dreamwork as a limitless process we develop a broader approach. This enables us to select from that pool of awareness at any given time and feel that it is a part of us and not just a dream. The acceptance of the dream self or dream ego in its various symbolic forms is important. If we do not accept the fact that it is us, we considerably reduce the chances of deriving any conscious benefit.

DREAMWORK WILL ONLY RAISE THE LEVEL OF CONSCIOUSNESS TO THE EXTENT THAT THE DREAMER MEETS THE TASK PRESENTED BY THE DREAM. DREAMS WILL ALWAYS POINT OUT WAYS IN WHICH YOU MAY ENRICH YOUR LIFE, BUT THIS USUALLY REQUIRES CHANGE— CHANGE OF APPROACH, DIRECTION, ATTITUDE, BEHAVIOR, VALUES AND ALL ELSE THAT HAS TO DO WITH ONESELF.

Sometimes when the dream student encounters this realization a form of resistance arises, like the inability to recall the previous night's dream. This type of censorship can continue for an incredibly long time, yet **"WHERE YOU RESIST THE DREAM WILL PERSIST,"** continuing to repeat itself in the hopes that it may be heard, attempting to reach us on some intuitive level and filter its way into our consciousness.

On the other hand, it is equally important for the dreamer not to set up any impossible tasks like attempting to interpret every night's dream or dreams. There is no quicker way to lose interest that I know. Dreamwork is like exercise. If you exercise in a gym, neither the gym nor its equipment will tone the body without the use of the muscles. We use the gym as an incentive, an initiative or an inspiration toward an end. It is the same with dreamwork where we exercise our intuitive and mental faculties. As our working knowledge of dreams increases and our intuition becomes stronger, we begin to understand our dreams more readily. In becoming more skillful, we recognize which dreams in particular are of greater importance. Initially, however, certain steps must be taken to train the mind in the language of dreams. Later chapters in this book will outline a procedure for those interested.

MOTIVE FOR DREAMING

We of the earth plane have chosen a particular path of evolution. Inherent within us is a deep longing for something we cannot describe, something neither fame, wealth nor material possessions can supply. It is an emptiness even those nearest to us cannot completely fill. Religion and a sound philosophy may help to ease that gap and the intellect may attempt to rationalize it away, but in essence all we have done is hide it deeper within ourselves. I am reminded of the story of three Buddhist monks who found illumination and attempted to keep it from humankind. In discussing where they should hide it, one said, "Let us hide it atop the highest mountain in the Himalayas. Surely no one will find it there."

"No," another monk said. "Let us hide it at the deepest part of the sea."

"You are both wrong," stated the third monk. "We must hide it in a place where man will never look."

"Where is that?" they both asked.

"Within himself," the third monk replied, at which they all agreed.

And so it is. Our spiritual evolution begins and ends with the self, a quest to find the lost Holy Grail or spiritual self buried deep within. An innate yearning drives us to integrate this missing element, so that we may become whole and complete beings. In viewing our dreams, we see many separate and distinct aspects all wanting to run off in different directions. By bringing them together in unison and harmony we accomplish the integration our dreams strive for. In one channeling session, I asked if there was a particular motive for dreaming. This is what I was given:

THE PREVAILING MOTIVE BEHIND DREAMS IS TO MOVE A PERSON SPIRITUALLY TOWARD HIS OR HER GOAL OF UNION WITH THE SOUL. THAT IS THE ONLY REASON FOR INTEGRATION AND INTEGRATION IS THE ONLY REASON FOR DREAMING. IN MOVING TOWARD THIS ULTI-MATE UNION, ONE HAS TO INTEGRATE DIFFER-ENT ASPECTS OF THE SELF, WHICH INVOLVES BECOMING MORE SENSITIVE TO THE SUR-ROUNDING SITUATIONS.

Lasting fulfillment is found through uniting with our soul. The masters, whose words are stated here, became so by mastering themselves. By delving deep into the dark recesses of their inner being and opening it up to the light, they conquered the limitations of the physical plane. We also have that choice, and will find a willing partner in our dreams if we choose to consciously deal with our limitations.

"What are the consequences when a person doesn't deal with a given situation consciously?" I once asked. "Does it have to be confronted on some level within the psyche in the dream state?"

AT SOME POINT IT MUST BE CONFRONTED, WHENEVER THAT AWARENESS, THE TIMING OF THAT AWARENESS WOULD FURTHER GROWTH TOWARD THE SOUL. IT DOES NOT ENTER INTO ONE'S DREAM LIFE AS A MESSAGE TO STOP

DOING SOMETHING PER SE, BUT IT WILL ENTER ON A PREDOMINANTLY FEARFUL THEME SUCH AS RUNNING FROM SOMETHING, ENCOUNTERING A FEARFUL FIGURE, FEELINGS OF DANGER OR SITUATIONS OF PERIL. THIS IS BECAUSE THE DREAMER HAS CHOSEN TO CONSCIOUSLY REMOVE THAT AWARENESS OUT OF FEAR, CONSEQUENTLY, IT REMAINS FESTERING WITHIN.

Conceivably it could be many years before the fear again arises within the dream state, providing us with the opportunity to gain in awareness. Presumably, when such a growth cycle does occur, it is triggered by an inner response and signals a reaching out for further development. Fearful, repetitive dreams are but symptomatic results, allowing the dreamer the opportunity for some positive developmental changes through confrontation. If we consciously work with our dreams the integration will take place much sooner than if we work only from an unconscious level. If, while doing dreamwork the dreamer consciously resists the message, it will be repeated in much the same manner as if the dreamer was unconscious of what was occurring. This holds true even if we accept the message but make no effort to work it out. Dream messages will continue until they have filtered and worked their way through the whole experience of the individual. A person who is resistant will have cycles of repetitive dreams over many years and perhaps an entire lifetime.

CHANNELING

Most of this information stems from channeled messages. Parting the veil, I would like to share with the reader what a typical session was like. Most often, it was on a one-to-one basis, although occasionally it was within the framework of a group. Much depends upon the particular channel's requirements. Some felt a group situation was distracting, preventing them from entering a trance deep enough to establish contact. The sessions always took place in a private home, usually that of the channel. My custom was to prepare a few basic questions in advance, along with several dreams in need of clearer interpretation. The individual to do the channeling would then make herself comfortable, either sitting or reclining.

With Beth, I used a standard hypnotic induction, continuing to a point where she signaled her readiness. All channels will give a signal when ready to be addressed. When this occurred, I would turn on the tape recorder and begin with my questions. If it was a group setting, we would take turns asking our questions.

The following is an example of one of my sessions with Beth. In this instance, the two of us were alone. I only submitted one dream for interpretation because of numerous other questions. Also, we attempted to maintain a time limit. Obviously, there was no way to tell in advance how many questions would be answered, as the initial answer usually prompted further inquiry. After the hypnotic induction brought Beth to a deep enough state, her guide would signal by stating: **"WE ARE NOW READY FOR QUESTIONS."** I then turned on the tape recorder and began with my first question:

I dreamt I stopped by this motel to get the price of a room. I asked the desk clerk if they were thirty-five dollars. He said no, thirty dollars was more like it, and thirty-four dollars would even include having the police stop by every hour or so. He asked if the room was for me and I said no, it was for someone I was expecting. I then noticed a large angelfish flying around the room. Surprised, I questioned him about it. He was rather casual in stating that he bought it when it was small and it always did that. The fish flew toward a spider on a web in the corner and ate it. After getting briefly caught in the web it broke free and flew away. Some jets in the floor were producing a fine spray of water that I felt the fish in some way utilized. The clerk noticed I had brought my gold recliner chair and a few other items that I had purchased at a secondhand store. I observed the motel was in a run-down condition, and wondered why I chose to go there.

YOU ARE SEEKING TO MOVE INTO A POSITION THAT WILL PAY THIRTY-FIVE THOUSAND DOL-LARS A YEAR. THIRTY THOUSAND IS MORE LIKELY. THIRTY-FOUR THOUSAND WOULD BUY A LOT OF SECURITY. YOU ARE EXPECTING EVENTUALLY TO HAVE A CHILD AND ANTICI-PATING THE EXTRA FINANCIAL BURDEN. THE ANGELFISH IS YOUR SPIRITUAL POTENTIAL, WHICH HAS ALWAYS BEEN WITH YOU. SEEING IT COMES AS A SURPRISE SINCE YOU HAVE FORGOTTEN ABOUT IT. THE SPIDER AND WEB ARE ASPECTS OF YOURSELF CAUGHT UP IN YOUR PROBLEMS. THIS IS SWALLOWED UP BY YOUR SPIRITUAL SIDE. THE ANGELFISH IS SUPPORTED BY YOUR INSPIRATION WHICH IS THE SPRAY FROM THE WATER JETS. THE GOLD CHAIR IS SECONDHAND INFORMATION RECEIVED FROM CHANNELED SESSIONS ON DREAMS. THE RUN-DOWN CONDITION OF THE MOTEL REFLECTS YOUR FEELINGS ABOUT YOUR CURRENT SITUATION IN LIFE.

Hardly a moment elapsed between the time I spoke the last word of my dream and the time the interpretation began. It felt completely right, a perfect reflection of my feelings. I looked down at Beth who, with her eyes closed in trance, lay back *in my gold recliner chair.* Since I had no further questions concerning that dream, I went on:

"If dreams contain messages of potential importance to us consciously, why is their rendering so complex?"

THEY ARE NOT ALWAYS SO COMPLEX. THE DREAM COMES IN VARIOUS STAGES AND YOU CAN EASILY PINPOINT WHAT STAGE A PERSON IS IN BY THE RELATIVE SIMPLICITY, VAGUENESS OR COMPLEXITY OF THE DREAM. IN SOME, THE FIRST PHASE IS THE VAGUE OR DIFFICULT-TO-REMEMBER DREAM WHERE THE INDIVIDUAL IS NOT DEVELOPING THAT PARTICULAR ASPECT THAT ALLOWS DREAMS TO COME FORTH EASILY. THIS IS ALSO TRUE IN PEOPLE WHO ARE RATHER UNDEVELOPED, CONCENTRATING ON A PERSONALITY LEVEL AND NOT PAYING ATTENTION TO THEIR INNER SIDE. THIS THEN CHANGES TO THE RELATIVELY COMPLEX DREAM WHERE A PERSON'S EXPERIENCE OF HIS OR HER INNER WORLD IS VASTLY COMPLICATED BY CONFUSION, WHERE THE INDIVIDUAL ALMOST COMPLETELY PROJECTS HIM OR HERSELF INTO THE OUTER WORLD. WHEN A PERSON BEGINS TO INTEGRATE THE INNER WITH THE OUTER EXPERIENCE THE COMPLEXITY OF THE DREAM WILL GIVE WAY TO INTENSITY. THIS IS WHERE THE DREAMER BEGINS TO GRAPPLE WITH DEEP INNER IMPULSES AND THE INTEGRATION PROCESS BECOMES INTENSE.

DREAMS BECOME INCREASINGLY SIMPLER AND MORE CONDENSED AS THESE IMPULSES BECOME INTEGRATED EITHER THROUGH DREAMWORK OR SOME OTHER PSYCHOLOGI-

CAL OR SPIRITUAL PROCESS. THE PHASE OF
DEVELOPMENT MAY BE CONSIDERED HIGH IN
A PERSON WHO HAS CLEAR DREAMS OF A
SIMPLE NATURE AND HAS NEVER BEEN
INVOLVED IN DREAMWORK. SIMPLER DREAMS
CONTAINING MORE CONDENSED MESSAGES
REQUIRE A MORE ADVANCED UNDERSTANDING
OF SYMBOLISM FOR THEIR INTERPRETATION.
THIS IS BECAUSE THEY ARE SO ENCAPSULATED,
PRIMARILY FROM THE MENTAL LEVEL. MUCH
MORE INSIGHT AND INFORMATION WILL COME
FROM YOUR OWN UNDERSTANDING ON A
DEEPER LEVEL, WHICH WILL EQUAL IF NOT
SURPASS THE INFORMATION YOU RECEIVE
FROM US.

"When you say the personality level do you mean the ego?"
I asked. "If so, can the ego directly influence the dream to
a noticeable extent?"

YES, YOU CAN HAVE AN EGO THAT IS STRONG
ENOUGH TO AFFECT THE DREAM LIFE QUITE
DRAMATICALLY. IT WILL BE BY EGOIC
IMPULSES THAT ARE NOT COMPLETELY CON-
SCIOUS AND CAN BE LOOKED UPON AS SUB-
CONSCIOUS INTERFERENCE. IT DOES NOT HAVE
TO BE A DREAM COMING FROM SOMETHING
NOT BEING ASSIMILATED BY THE DREAMER,
EXCEPT PERHAPS ON SOME EGOIC LEVEL. IN
THIS INSTANCE YOU WILL FIND THE INDIVID-
UAL DREAMING ABOUT PEOPLE ALL THE TIME.
THIS IS MOST COMMON IN TEEN-AGERS WHERE
THEY DREAM OF SEEING THIS PERSON AND
GOING OUT WITH THAT PERSON, PARTYING,
SHOPPING, ETC. DREAMS COMING COM-

PLETELY FROM THE SUBCONSCIOUS, THAT IS, WITHOUT EGOIC INFLUENCE ARE NOT QUITE SO MUNDANE.

CONSEQUENTLY, WHEN YOU HAVE DREAMS THAT ARE FAIRLY MUNDANE CONSISTENTLY, AND YOU DON'T HAVE THAT MANY UNUSUAL SYMBOLS, IT IS THEN SAFE TO SAY THERE IS A STRONG EGOIC INFLUENCE AT WORK AFFECTING THE DREAMS. IT ALSO INDICATES THAT A PERSON IS NOT EXPERIENCING THE DEEPER LEVEL OF HIS OR HER INCARNATION AT THIS TIME. THIS, HOWEVER, WILL RUN IN CYCLES. EVEN A PERSON WITH A VERY STRONG EGO WILL HAVE PHASES OF POWERFUL DREAMS THAT REFLECT THE DEEPER SIDE OF THEIR NATURE. THIS OCCURRENCE USUALLY EVOKES A NEGATIVE REACTION FROM THE DREAMER BECAUSE HE OR SHE IS UNCOMFORTABLE WITH THE UNFAMILIAR. THIS CAN BE SEEN FOR EXAMPLE IN HEATHER'S [a student] DREAMS. SOMETIMES THEY WILL COME THROUGH ON A LESS EGOIC LEVEL AS SEEN WITH HER DREAM WITH THE PUMPKINS—A SEASONAL SYMBOL THAT DOES NOT OCCUR JUST ANYTIME. HER OTHER DREAMS, HOWEVER—RIDING IN A CAR, TALKING WITH FRIENDS, GOING TO A PARTY AND MORE TALKING—YOU WILL FIND THAT OVER AND OVER AGAIN. EXAMINE YOUR STUDENTS' MATERIAL, EVEN THE DIFFERENT GROUPS AT LARGE. YOU WILL FIND SOME FAR MORE EGOICALLY BOUND THAN OTHERS.

"When we wake up grouchy in the morning is it because of a dream that reflected something we didn't like?"

IN THE TYPE OF PERSON WE WERE DISCUSSING, THE FAIRLY EGOICALLY BOUND ONE, NO. THEY ARE NOT IN TOUCH ENOUGH WITH THEIR INNER SELVES TO BE THAT AFFECTED BY A DREAM THEY DON'T LIKE. ALSO, THEY ARE QUITE CAPABLE OF REPRESSING IT. NOW, THE MORE SENSITIVE THEY ARE TO THEIR INNER EXPERIENCE, THE MORE THEY WILL BE AFFECTED BY THEIR DREAM LIFE. THE EXCEPTION WOULD BE WHEN A PERSON OF ANY LEVEL OF AWARENESS RECEIVES A PROFOUND WARNING. THIS WILL TEND TO UPSET ANYONE. YOU WILL NOTE THAT PEOPLE WHO ARE SENSITIVE TO THEIR INNER EXPERIENCE WILL REACT TO A DREAM IN MUCH THE SAME WAY AS THEY WOULD HAD THE EXPERIENCE OCCURRED IN THEIR WAKING LIFE. THIS IS BECAUSE IT IS JUST AS REAL AND A PART OF THEM AS THEIR TANGIBLE DAY-TO-DAY EXISTENCE. IT IS IN FACT A HEALTHY SIGN WHEN SOMEONE REACTS EMOTIONALLY TO A DISTURBING DREAM, AS THAT MAY BE USED AS AN INDICATOR TOWARD THEIR SENSITIVITY.

"You mentioned earlier about dreams emerging directly from the subconscious mind as opposed to those which are egoically influenced. Don't egoically influenced dreams also come from the subconscious?"

YES, IN "A COURSE IN MIRACLES" DREAMS ARE EXPLAINED IN THE MOST PROFOUND AND BROADEST MANNER POSSIBLE. YOU DREAM AS LONG AS YOU PERCEIVE; ONCE YOU KNOW, YOU DO NOT DREAM. DREAMS ARE A PRODUCT OF PERCEIVING AND PERCEPTION IS A PRODUCT

OF DUALITY WITHIN THE SELF. DREAMS
EMERGE FROM AN UNCONSCIOUS SOURCE
BECAUSE THAT IS THE ULTIMATE MANNER IN
WHICH TO EXPRESS THE SEPARATION
BETWEEN MAN'S CONSCIOUS AND UNCONS-
CIOUS NATURE.

"What you're saying, then, is that as a person becomes more
fully integrated, their sense of duality lessens and so they dream
less."

MASTERS DO NOT DREAM. IN FACT, ADEPTS ARE
NOT PARTICULARLY KNOWN FOR THEIR DREAM
STATES EITHER. MOST OF THE TIME THEY ARE
DESCRIBED AS ECSTATIC, MEDITATIVE OR OUT-
OF-BODY STATES. YOU MAY FIND ABSTRACT
COMMUNICATION TAKING PLACE IN A DREAM-
LIKE MANNER, BUT THAT IS NOT THE INTEG-
RATIVE PROCESS WE CALL DREAMING. SO, YOU
CAN SEE VERY CLEARLY THE DISTINCTION
BETWEEN THOSE ALREADY QUITE EVOLVED, TO
THOSE VERY MUCH IN NEED OF THE INTEGRA-
TIVE CAPACITY OF THE DREAM, TO THOSE WHO
HAVE ALREADY INTEGRATED TO THE POINT
WHERE THEY HAVE ABSOLUTELY NO NEED TO
DREAM.

"A while ago, you mentioned the egoic dreams of teen-
agers. Could you elaborate a little more on childhood dreams?"

THE ROLE OF CHILDREN IS PERHAPS THE MOST
DIFFICULT TO EXPLAIN IN TERMS OF INTEGRA-
TION. CHILDHOOD DREAMS ARE REFLECTIVE
OF THE EMOTIONAL EXPERIENCE OF THE
CHILD. AT THIS STAGE, EMOTIONAL DEVELOP-

MENT IS TAKING PLACE. BY AND LARGE CHILD-
REN DO NOT PAY ANY ATTENTION TO HOW THEY
ARE FEELING. FEELING AND LIVING OR FEEL-
ING AND EXPERIENCING ARE VERY MUCH THE
SAME THING WITH CHILDREN. IT DOES NOT
OCCUR TO THEM TO IDENTIFY WITH THEIR
FEELINGS, NOR DO THEY REALIZE SUCH FEEL-
INGS EVEN EXIST. BECAUSE IT IS ALMOST
COMPLETELY SUBCONSCIOUS, IT MUST BE
WORKED OUT WITHIN THE PSYCHE. THERE IS
A VERY STRONG DEMAND HEALTHWISE FOR
THIS TO TAKE PLACE. SO YOU WILL HAVE
CHILDREN DREAMING ABOUT THEIR EXPE-
RIENCES MOST OF THE TIME.

INFANCY IS DIFFERENT BECAUSE THE FEEL-
INGS ARE NOT QUITE AS DEVELOPED. IT
BECOMES MORE OF A PRIMAL EXPERIENCE,
AND IN SOME, IT IS MORE OF A SPIRITUAL
EXPERIENCE BECAUSE INFANTS ARE STILL
CONNECTED TO A MORE UNIVERSAL SENSE OF
THEIR DREAMS—MANIPULATING THE INNER
SYMBOLS WITH THE OUTER WORLD, AND
BEGINNING TO INTEGRATE THE TWO. WHEN
INFANTS DREAM, THEY ARE COORDINATING
THEIR SOUL OR INNER LIFE PLAN TO THEIR
ENVIRONMENT. THIS OCCURS ON A VERY
ABSTRACT LEVEL.

THE ADOLESCENT STAGE IS MUCH MORE
COMPLEX. A TRANSITION OF THE DREAM
THEME WILL PARALLEL THE TRANSITION
FROM THE CHILDHOOD TO ADOLESCENCE,
SHIFTING TOWARD MORE COMPLEX SITUA-
TIONS AND OUTER EXPERIENCES IN THE SAME
MANNER AS AN ADULT. THE EXCEPTION IS
THAT THE ISSUES ARE NOT AS COMPLEX. OF

COURSE, AND THIS IS CHARACTERISTIC OF ANY AGE GROUP, IF THE SECURITY IS IN SOME WAY THREATENED, THE DREAMS WILL TAKE ON A DISTURBING QUALITY WHICH COULD APPEAR TO BE HIGHLY ABSTRACT. ANOTHER TIME IS DURING THE TRANSITION STAGE AROUND THE AGES OF TWELVE TO FOURTEEN, WHEN THEY EXPERIENCE MANY ARCHETYPAL DREAMS. AFTER THAT PERIOD, DREAMS WILL REVOLVE AROUND BASIC ISSUES OCCURRING IN THAT PERSON'S LIFE AT THE TIME. THERE WILL NOT BE ANY ABSTRACT OR HIGHLY SYMBOLIC DREAMS UNLESS THE TEEN-AGER IS EITHER DEEPLY DISTURBED OR HIGHLY EVOLVED. THE MORE COMPLEX DREAMS OF ADULTHOOD EMERGE ABOUT THE AGES OF EIGHTEEN TO TWENTY-ONE, WHEN THE MENTAL IS MORE FULLY DEVELOPED.

"What about the dreams of the mentally disturbed? Can you tell us anything about them?"

IN REGARD TO DREAMS OF THE NEUROTIC OR PSYCHOTIC . . . THESE BEINGS ARE NOT OPEN. THEY DO NOT CHANNEL HIGHER ENERGIES BECAUSE THEIR STATE HAS THEM IN A RATHER CLOSED OR DARK LEVEL. THEY CAN BE PSY-CHIC AND INSIGHTFUL, BUT THEIR RECEPTIV-ITY IS USUALLY FROM THE LOWER ASTRAL. A DREAM ESSENTIALLY PULLS FROM THE SPIR-ITUAL LIFE OF AN INDIVIDUAL BECAUSE THE DREAM IS MOVING THEM ON TOWARD SPIRIT-UAL PROGRESS, THAT IS ITS PURPOSE. BUT WHEN YOU HAVE A PERSON WHOSE INCARNA-TION IS IN SPIRITUAL DARKNESS, SO TO SPEAK,

YOU WILL NOT HAVE THE SAME TYPE OF INFLUENCE COMING FROM THEIR DREAMS. RATHER, YOU WILL HAVE AN ATTEMPT TO WORK OUT THE INFLUENCES WITHIN THE PERSON AS OPPOSED TO AN ABILITY TO LEAD OR DIRECT. WHAT THEY ARE EXPERIENCING HAS SO OVERWHELMED THEM THAT ALL THEY CAN DO IS WORK OUT FURTHER IN THEIR DREAM LIFE WHAT THEY ARE EXPERIENCING IN THEIR PHYSICAL REALITY—A SAD STATE INDEED.

Seeing our time was short, I decided to end the session. Thanking the entity, I stated I had no more questions and asked if there were any closing words. This time there were none, and I was graciously thanked in turn as the being withdrew. Using appropriate suggestions, I gently brought Beth back to a cognitive state. Like most trance channels, her memory of what transpired was foggy at best. Soon she would lose most of what she now retained. Those who use self-hypnosis or deep meditation and bring themselves out on their own are usually more cognizant and have better retention.

Afterward, we discussed the information we received. If it was within the context of a group, it was usually a lively discussion as the energy level would be quite high. Later, in quiet solitude, I would study the material in depth . . . finding answers to questions I had not even thought to ask.

2

Symbols:
The Language of
Dreams

Symbols are signs inferring something other than what they illustrate. Expressing meaningful and sometimes profound information, they are a direct and condensed form of communication—a language expressly more efficient than our present cumbersome method of dialogue. Symbols are difficult to understand, and because of this some claim they are purposefully veiled. Yet symbols are the language of the universe, a part of the natural order of things. This was much better understood in ages past, when people lived closer to the earth.

The further back we delve into our history, the more we find the use of symbols. Petroglyphs painted on a cave wall chronicle the story of a great hunt. Some Egyptian hieroglyphics carved on a mummy's tomb tell of the reign of a notable pharaoh. Mythological stories of ancient Greece revolve around human passions, strengths and weaknesses. The scriptures of most religions are symbolic in content, including the parables spoken by Jesus as recorded in the New Testament. American Indians and others in harmony with the land could read the symbols of nature, while astrologers read the symbols of the stars.

Most of us are familiar with the Biblical story of the Tower of Babel.[1] It told of a time when all the people of the earth had a common language. I believe it may have been a symbolic one. My interpretation of this allegorical tale is this: Motivated by greed, we attempted to reach a false paradise built upon material desires, causing us to lose the bond we held with each other, as well as with our Creator. We went away babbling in "tongues," unable to understand one another. Today, speaking the same language, we are still unable to understand one another.

Essentially, I believe we have cut ourselves off from the divine aspect within, and in doing so consciously lost a form of symbolic communication that granted us valuable guidance. In addition, we lost the ability to communicate sensitively and intelligently among ourselves. This has cost the human race dearly, as history can attest. By developing a greater degree of sensitivity gained through self-awareness, however, we can reverse this position. Only a sensitively attuned individual can read the deeper meanings of symbols, and we begin by becoming sensitive to ourselves. Dreams attempt to help us gain personal awareness—like waves pounding against a rock, they repeatedly try to raise our consciousness—pointing out ways in which we may broaden our insight.

Dream symbols are mostly personal and can alternately assume different meanings. We create a personal symbol by forming an association with events or conditions arising from a given set of circumstances. An impression, often connected to our feelings, becomes transformed into a symbol. Because our feelings and attitudes are always changing, a personal symbol can never have a fixed meaning. A "dog" for instance, may represent a member of the opposite sex who the dreamer finds unattractive. If the dreamer is "dog tired" then the dog may characteristically symbolize how the dreamer is physically feeling. A playful dog can represent one's playful feelings.

Such symbols also reach out beyond the obvious feeling level. For example, when the dog's role is that of a protector or guardian, it could possibly signify unseen guidance or intuition. Also, a dog that appears menacing can represent a threat such as an illness the dreamer might be facing. Consequently, a personal dream symbol, derived from an association formed by the dreamer and brought to life in the dream, can represent any number of things.

Other symbols are of a more general nature. A *key* for instance, represents a *clue* which may *unlock* something. A *letter* symbolizes a *message*, while a *telephone* may symbolize both a *message* and *communication*. Such symbols have more widespread meanings than personal symbols.

THE ARCHETYPE

On a deeper level lies the universal symbolism of the archetype.[2] Jung calls this level the *collective unconscious.*[3] It contains the primal content of the racial unconscious, consisting of *inherited ideas and predispositions.* An archetype, having a fixed meaning, is a blueprint or prototype, a parent model whose offspring are lesser symbols of the same type. Many of the lesser symbols in dreams can be traced back to their archetypal parents who have a broader and more profound meaning. In dreamwork, when this is done we call it *amplification.*

We can amplify many dreams to the archetypal level. Jung felt that on this level mythology plays a strong role, as the gods, demigods and other assorted creatures correspond to the many aspects of our human qualities. The Greek goddess Aphrodite and her Roman counterpart Venus, for instance, are ultimate symbols of our romantic love nature, and therefore considered archetypes. A lesser dream symbol could appear more literally as the actual person with whom we are romantically involved. Dancing, music, flowers and valentines are all romantic symbols which can be amplified to the archetypal level of Venus or Aphrodite. Jesus, the archetype of brotherly love and forgiveness, symbolizes the Christ within and spiritual guidance for the Christian. To the Buddhist, Buddha would archetypally represent The Four Noble Truths, or the essence of the Noble Eightfold Path.

Purely archetypal dreams are usually related only abstractly to personal experiences, having an intrinsic meaning correlating to a universal pattern found in the collective unconscious. Such dreams—said to occur primarily during critical phases of our life such as puberty, midlife and toward the end of our life—are quite far-reaching. Metaphysical thought contends such dreams can also be an overview, focusing upon particular areas of one's life corresponding to similar past life experiences. They may function as a summation or perhaps a completion of certain lessons that may have been going on for many incarnations. In metaphysical terms we call it a *round*.

Incarnating in groups, we learn and experience on both an individual and group level. The same group of people continues to reincarnate together over a long period, collectively sharing their experiences on a soul level. The collective unconscious is of course strongly receptive to this mass input. Eventually we complete the cycle, thus concluding a round. A group unit begins with the immediate family and moves upward to include communities, states or provinces, nations and finally, the entire human race—all providing energy (creating and reinforcing patterns) to the collective unconscious.

RACE MIND

The collective unconscious in some respects parallels what early Mystery School teachings call the *Race Mind,*[4] containing our collective memory dating back to creation. What we do not quite realize is how strongly it influences us. Modern psychology has focused deeply upon a primal level, studying the effects or imprint of that level upon our psyche. However, due consideration must be given to the present, and how current thinking influences the masses. The race mind as a collective memory is like a pool of humankind's thoughts, feelings and beliefs. Our personal contribution to the race mind is reflected in our own archetypal dreams, depicting our traits, beliefs, fears, superstitions, drives and ambitions—the depth of which serves to illustrate the degree of our present individual and collective state of evolution.

Certain metaphysical schools recognize the archetype, but in contrast to Jung's theory, they believe it to be an embodiment of lesser thoughtforms having a similar pattern; a collection of comparable thoughts banded together and forming a composite. Belief has it we contribute to the activity of these archetypal forms by adding our own personal thoughts and attitudes to their store. This collective level contains every worthwhile thought imparted by humanity. It is also a receptacle of our fears, prejudices, greed and hatred. Similar to a bank, it contains both positive and negative deposits upon which we may unconsciously draw. Every great personage has deposited his or her thought essence into this pool, which can be drawn upon in moments of need. Conversely, the worst minds have also deposited their thoughts here. When we become immersed in anger and bitterness, we unconsciously open ourselves to these negative energies.

Whenever we feel strongly about one thing or another we tap into this bank, which in turn subtly tends to reinforce our feelings. Drawing from the collected thoughts of others before us, we are swayed by their influence in much the same manner as a mob is influenced by the thoughts it generates. The input from society dictates an ever changing pattern, and to become caught up in such a pattern is said to be influenced in part by *mass consciousness*, that is, swayed by the beliefs of the masses and echoing their sentiments while believing them to be ours.

At higher frequencies thoughts have a pattern or shape, and like all wavelengths, they reflect color and emit a resonance. For this reason, we call them thoughtforms. Edgar Cayce gave a beautiful description of the power of thought in one reading:

> "For mind is the builder and that which we think about may become crimes or miracles. For thoughts are things and as their currents run through the environs of an entity's experience thoughts become barriers or stepping stones, depending upon the manner in which the thoughts are laid out as it were. For as the mental dwells upon these thoughts, so does it give it strength, power to things that do not appear. And thus does indeed there become that as is so oft given, that faith is the evidence of things not seen." (906-3) [5]

In essence, the mind gives strength to what it dwells upon, mobilizing invisible forces to action. The forces that inhabit the race mind are alive in a sense, empowered by our collective emotions and feelings to inspire and uplift us, or bring us havoc and chaos.

YIN AND YANG

The most common archetypal figures can be found in the appearance of the anima and the animus. I prefer to use the terms yin and yang. Strictly speaking, the anima refers to feminine side of the male while the animus is the masculine side of the female. Yin and yang however, refer to masculine or feminine polarity without regard to sex. The yin, considered to be characteristic of the emotional nature of the female, is sensual, passive and sensitively receptive. The yang embraces reason, logic, forcefulness, aggressiveness and physical sensation. Water and earth are feminine symbols, while the elements of fire and air are masculine. The yin, negative in polarity (as in electricity), is magnetic. She rules the stars, the moon and the night, including all that is hidden, mysterious and obscure. The unconscious and subconscious, the psychic, love and romance, coolness, jealousy, intuition, nurturance, fertility and inactivity are all relegated to the feminine, yin side.

The yang or positive polarity is electric, encompassing the sun, air, fire, light, expansion, dominance, anger, violence, activity, heat, expansion, passion and sex. Each polarity has both constructive and destructive qualities and it is easy to see how unbalanced we become by leaning too far in either direction. An insecure, jealous, secretive and wily female would be considered strongly yin, as would a loving homebody type that likes romantic novels, poetry and flowers. An outgoing, assertive female who likes camping, horseback riding and sports would be considered quite yang.

Metaphysics considers the soul to be androgynous, consisting of both yin and yang components, while its extension in human form assumes the role of one sex or the other. Two factors determine the choice of sex while in physical incarnation, the foremost being karma, incurred from a past life. If the individual committed an offense toward a member or members of the opposite sex in a prior incarnation, they may choose to return in the form of the offended sex, creating conditions similar in nature to those past in order to experience what it is like to be in the other person's shoes. Such a judgment and consequent *sentence* takes place in one's psyche, and is not meted out by some outside influence as many would believe. An internal response mechanism, it is a product of our own judgmental nature and directly corresponds to our own prejudices.

On the other hand, we may choose the role of a particular sex for the express purpose of integrating certain innate qualities which that sex can provide. An overly yang male might incarnate as a female in order to experience and integrate particular yin attributes to help balance out the polarity. Such a female might show evidence of her male past life or lives through her personality makeup, and in some cases, through sexual preferences.

While in incarnation, we sense the lack or "incompleteness" of our opposite side. Our longing to integrate this component takes on the form of a sexual need, a desire to merge or bond with the opposite sex. Sexual intercourse is symbolic of uniting with our missing half, providing a temporary semblance of what it is like to feel complete. On another level, it symbolizes the soul's aspiration or goal of unification. In becoming more integrated, the physical need for sex lessens accordingly, as part of our natural evolutionary process. When we reach the final stage of our spiritual evolution and our integration is complete, the desire for sexual union subsides. Some religious orders emulate this stage by prematurely taking vows of celibacy, signifying spiritual completeness.

In studying the content of our dream material we can readily assign each symbol a yin or yang attribute, enabling us to ascertain which polarity is being affected. We may then seek to uncover what inner quality is attempting to integrate, or is in need of integration. Since integration serves to balance our polarity, everything we integrate must have either a masculine or feminine characteristic. By balancing these inner forces, we transform destructive traits into positive qualities. Anger, for instance, usually arises when someone or something does not conform to what **WE** want. When directed either outwardly to another, or inwardly towards oneself it is a glaring example of unforgiveness. Because it has an outward thrust that blocks our yin attribute of receptivity, it is considered a yang characteristic. Anger, whose element is fire, is of course equally shared by both sexes. Earth and water are its opposites. The earth element produces a stabilizing condition while water tranquilizes, quenches and cools. By introducing these yin qualities of stability and tranquility, we achieve an integration by neutralization, thus restoring our necessary balance.

Forcefulness or aggressive behavior, a negative yang trait, can be transformed into a positive type of assertiveness, used to promote self-discipline and motivation. In this instance, by modifying or tempering one's aggressive nature with sensitivity (a yin quality), we retain our power without being pushy or domineering. Sex without love is an imbalance of the yang side, while meekness or timidness is an imbalance of the yin. In one instance, we have a one-sided masculine quality in need of feminine balance, while the other is just the opposite. These qualities, often played out by appropriate male or female figures in a dream, convey the yin or yang role seeking integration.

The sex of the dream figure, as well as the use of masculine or feminine symbols found in the dream, tells us what qualities (yin or yang) are being integrated or are seeking integration. The side in need of balance will usually play the dominant role, essentially telling the dreamer where to focus. Subconscious or unconscious elements will always assume a yin role such as a cat, a body of water, the submerged portion of an iceberg, Africa (The Dark Continent), and for many Caucasians a black person. Yang symbols are automobiles, machinery and most instruments (other than musical or artistic). Creative talent, the healing arts, and nature are yin. Yet within these broad categories, we again find yin and yang divisions. Metals for example, fall into the yang category, yet silver is considered yin while gold is yang. Often the symbol used in a dream to indicate the polarity will also reveal the specific yin or yang trait. An attacking lioness would symbolize an *aggressive* yin aspect, either literally or symbolically. That is, it could represent a person in the dreamer's life or an aggressively emerging female characteristic.

While writing this book, my guides told me I needed more exercise. I began taking short walks, but evidently that was not enough, for soon thereafter I had the following dream:

GAY RAY

I dreamt I met and was warmly greeted by a very old friend of mine. In reality, he was somewhat of a soft, pudgy individual, but in the dream his shirt was off and he was very well-muscled. Marveling at his physique, I asked Ray if he worked out. Admitting that he did, he proceeded to show me his exercise room, complete with a bench, weights and other equipment. He then began to make "advances" toward me. Embarrassed, I told him I was not inclined that way, and quickly left.

While not exactly "soft and pudgy," it's been at least six months since I've physically worked out. Obviously, the dream was saying I needed to get back into a serious exercise routine. What I wish to point out here is the manner in which the dream addressed the issue. First, there was not one yin symbol in the entire dream. Second, Ray was certainly trying to "integrate" with me, pointing out the need to integrate some yang quality or characteristic. Through my writing, I have greatly strengthened my creative yin side, but only at the expense of my physical or yang. In the past, I exercised regularly, but during the course of writing this book *I was not inclined that way.* The dream's message to incorporate more exercise into my life was clear. Presently, there is not enough attention given to focusing on dreams as a source for providing insight into the nature of a polarity imbalance.

Another example concerns a dream student having two cats. One was a timid male, afraid of his own shadow. The other, a female, was just the opposite. She was outgoing, assertive and demanded attention. We discovered that in this person's dreams the male cat represented her fears, while the other symbolized her ambition to advance her career. This somewhat passive young woman earned a law degree while working as a secretary. However, she put off studying for her bar exam because she felt she lacked the assertive and aggressive character required for such a profession. Fearing she was too easily intimidated to be a capable attorney, her alternative would be corporate work, which she felt was dull and uninteresting. Unable to reach a decision, she remained stagnating in her present, low-paying position. Yet her dreams indicated that beneath her meek exterior lay the very qualities she felt were lacking. She needed to get past her dominating yin fears, which overshadowed her yang side.

Now if we amplify the cat or feline to the archetypal level we find it to be yin, and we know that fear and the subconscious are both yin. Inwardly, we have a conflict between her desires and the fear that she is incapable of having those desires realized. To integrate or resolve this problem, she needs to introduce the yang quality of assertiveness, thus enabling her to take the initiative and strive toward reaching her goal. Her dreams are saying she needs to assert herself first, developing more self-confidence as she goes.

On the surface, her dreams appear to be reflective of a conflict over feelings of inadequacy. However, there are indications of deeper issues involved. The symbols in her dreams are all yin. Two cats suggest a double or strong yin. The weak male and strong female suggest a dominating yin aspect. Now, let us assume this individual finds the courage to leave her present position and pursue the career she desires. Let us also assume this is an important decision on a soul level because she lost her self-confidence several incarnations back, and has been slowly working up to this point ever since. A pivotal point in her life now becomes a major soul growth issue. By relinquishing her fears she allows her yang side to reclaim its former position, enabling her to become a more balanced individual. The problems she confronted (created) were only incidental, planned out in advance as something to face and overcome. They allow her an opportunity to regain her former power by integrating particular yang qualities. Her advancement is then primarily a spiritual one, with positive ramifications extending to all levels of her life.

Unconcerned with personal issues of the dreamer, archetypal levels focus only upon the "essence" of what the dreamer contributes to the collective. This is why such dreams are rather impersonal, reflecting our contribution only in terms of how it affects the total condition. An archetypal dream presents a part of the overall picture regarding the balance of our collective human polarities. In the above example, the essence was fear. Overcoming that fear ever so slightly strengthened the balance of humankind's collective thoughts, providing a diminutive shift through integration.

Pivotal points in a person's life usually have to do with spiritual or "growth" issues. In this instance, a correspondence was made from the dreamer's fears to the fears lurking within all humankind, resulting in an archetypal dream that only remotely has to do with the dreamer, but to which the dreamer has contributed. There are many levels to a dream and its symbols. It is as if there are symbols contained within symbols, each correspondently interconnected, yet having a somewhat different meaning at different levels of consciousness.

ANONYMOUS FIGURES

On occasion we will find anonymous figures in our dreams. A stranger who plays a minor or supporting role, portraying either a masculine or feminine character. The age of the character often represents a level of maturity. For example, immature figures of boys or girls suggest undeveloped aspects of the dreamer. The more mature figures can either mean developing or fully developed aspects, including those which are excessively strong and perhaps attempting to take over. With males, we find the masculine traits of strength, domineering qualities and a thrusting out into the world. Involving a sense of self-confidence, it also includes various attempts at self-expression. With the female aspect the feelings tend to be more inward, such as negative feelings toward oneself, or sorrow or grief. Aspects of inner nurturance, creativity and a soft, gentle nature are also significant of the feminine polarity.

Anonymous figures are usually symbols telling us what qualities we are working with in terms of integration. A male student in one of my classes puzzled over a dream he was attempting to analyze. Hal had just completed his finals and was planning to move on to postgraduate work at an out-of-state university. Although the final grades were not yet posted, his high grade average assured his success. His dream is as follows:

I dreamt there were three sisters, and I was going with one of them. For some reason, I was attracted to another one and we somehow wound up having sex. After we finished the other two came in the house. One went into the kitchen and the other who was supposedly my girlfriend sat down next to me and asked if I had "made it" with her sister. She seemed somewhat teary eyed, as if she was hoping I hadn't. I comfort her and she starts to calm down. Now my real girlfriend is there and is telling me that these three are my assistants. There is a waterfall outside and I can hear it splashing in the background. I ask her jokingly if she can hear the wine being poured.

Since the sisters are the key to the dream, let us begin with them. Three anonymous figures that represent yin qualities. The fact that they are sisters signifies closely related issues. One had been "integrated," one was "sorrowful," and the other was in the "kitchen." Knowing Hal was a very creative and talented individual, I sought out his creative aspect, finding her in the kitchen where we "cook up" or "create" things. The "sad" sister could literally symbolize his girlfriend who would be unable to accompany him out-of-state. She could also represent his feelings over leaving his friends and school. The sister with whom he had sex could well represent his accomplishment, the result of academic integration, gained both through assimilation and creative application.

His real girlfriend played a cameo role in a sense, suggesting by her brief appearance that she was *a part of the picture.* His "assistants," as she called them, suggests *assistance.* This could well represent assistance that would someday benefit them both. As an art major, his was a yin field. If the three sisters represented his creative talent or ability, they would definitely be lending assistance. Moreover, the message to the effect that *he made it* was a good indication that he would pass. The pouring of wine further emphasized this, as it usually means a celebration is in order.

Hal felt good with the interpretation and admitted having "mixed feelings" about leaving, even if it was only to be temporary. The night before, he had been consoling his girlfriend, and pointed out that the plans cooked up in the kitchen could possibly be the future plans he and his girlfriend had been making concerning their relationship. Since romance is definitely yin, I did not rule out this possibility.

ASPECTS

While dream characters for the most part portray aspects of ourselves, occasionally they can be taken literally. You may dream about your employer at work and in a general sense he or she may literally represent your boss or some authority figure. It is also possible that dreaming about your job directly involves something going on at work. More likely, however, the dream revolves around something you are *working on.* The boss could be the aspect of yourself that has initiated or is overseeing this task. To dream of an ex-lover or former spouse for example, rarely has to do with them directly. Often, it suggests a parallel or similar experience presently occuring on some level within your current relationship.

Dream dynamics often revolve around the roles we assume in undertaking our responsibilities, primarily in the areas of relationships and career. While it is difficult to imagine a friend or relative, let alone an animal, portraying an aspect of ourselves, they all represent personal characteristics in most of our dreams. Whether these characters are a source of inspiration or exasperation, they portray a feeling or trait of the dreamer. To become adept at dream interpretation, one must thoroughly understand the nature of an aspect. **An aspect is always a trait, characteristic or feeling of the dreamer projected by the dream mind onto someone or something else.** A vase, for instance, usually represents a vessel or receptacle of the dreamer, reflective of one's physical, emotional, mental or spiritual contents, or any combination thereof. The vase is portraying some aspect of the dreamer.

An aspect is a symbol representing a particular side of the dreamer and is usually *both* the dreamer (in the dream) and whatever or whomever else the dreamer is associating with. If the secondary aspect is a figure familiar to the dreamer, it may represent a quality the dreamer has associated with this person in waking life, commonly having to do with their name, trade or profession, or even a personality trait. To make it even more confusing, a relative may signify a feeling or matter *in close relationship* to the dreamer, possibly a characteristic that they both share. One must thoroughly study the content of the dream material to arrive at the proper interpretation of an aspect.

Aspects portray a certain side of us, a side that takes on

a life of its own in a dream. They often personify feelings we have about the roles we play in our lives and their effects upon the lives of others. The areas where we live out our dramas and play our particular roles are said to be similar to little theaters. We portray one character in our parent-and-child relationship, another in our employee-and-employer relationship, and yet another in our mate or lover relationship. A relationship is even possible with something as general as a project or undertaking. Any particular activity can appear as a character in your dream, personifying your feelings connected to that activity. Characters in our dreams run the full gamut of our imagination, from the mundane to the outrageous, from the most fearful to the most humorous. The following dream is an example:

> *I dreamt Adele telephoned me, saying that she had lost a lot of weight while on her new diet and exercise program. I thought this was great and invited her over. When she arrived at my doorstep I was surprised to see that instead of being slimmer, she was about a foot and a half shorter and still the same shape.*

This dream student felt she was ignoring a weight problem. The demands on her life left little time to pursue the type of weight-loss program she desired. She and her friend Adele, who was also overweight, had been talking about diets and exercise programs the day before. Her dream was telling her she was feeling *shortchanged* instead of *slim-changed.* "I" in a dream is perhaps the most important clue we can uncover since it usually literally reveals the dreamer's feelings or activities. Often, it means "I am" or "I represent," so that Adele's exclamation *"I lost a lot of weight"* can be interpreted to mean "I am or I represent weight-loss." The dreamer's response was enthusiastic, again underscoring her desire to lose weight. The last sentence reveals her inner feelings, which turn up on her doorstep and are presented quite humorously. A common mistake in deciphering a dream is to focus too strongly on the character at the expense of the character's role. One might have spent considerable time trying to associate many different aspects to Adele. The main key or keys is often found in the first sentence: *weight, diet and exercise,* all pointing to the dreamer's weight problem. The last sentence underscores her inability to resolve it.

ANIMALS

The most common dream character other than a human figure is that of an animal. I once asked why we choose animals as symbols in our dreams. Here is their reply:

THE CHOOSING OF A SYMBOL OCCURS ON A LEVEL THAT IS INCOMPREHENSIBLE TO THE CONCRETE MIND, YET THE ABSTRACT MIND IS PERFECTLY COMFORTABLE AND AWARE OF THE PROCESS INVOLVED. ON AN INTELLECTUAL LEVEL AN EXPLANATION OF HOW PARTICULAR SYMBOLS ARE CHOSEN IS A FORMIDABLE TASK, MAINLY BECAUSE WE ARE DEALING IN A TIMELESS REALM WHEN WE DEAL WITH DREAMS. WHEN THE CHOICE FACTOR IS VIEWED FROM A PERSPECTIVE OF TIME, THERE IS A MULTITUDE OF SYMBOLS THAT MAY BE USED, EACH WITH MULTIPLE MEANINGS AND MULTIPLE WAYS OF BEING PRESENTED. YOUR QUESTION BASICALLY IS, HOW DO THEY SIFT DOWN INTO A SPECIFIC DREAM? FIRST YOU MUST VIEW THE DREAM AS A REFLECTION OF YOUR PHYSICAL OR ASTRAL LIFE. IT IS NOT SOMETHING THAT IS MERELY BROUGHT FROM THE UNCONSCIOUS TO THE CONSCIOUS, BUT

SOMETHING THAT OCCURRED FIRST IN THE PHYSICAL OR ASTRAL REALM, WAS ASSIMILATED BY THE UNCONSCIOUS AND IS NOW BEING RETRIEVED BY THE CONSCIOUS.

A SYMBOL IS DRAWN FROM AN OCCURRENCE, USUALLY THE DAY'S EVENTS. EACH SIGNIFICANT OCCURRENCE THAT TAKES PLACE IN YOUR LIFE BECOMES A SYMBOLIC EPISODE; THAT IS, IT HAS A DEEPER MEANING ON OTHER LEVELS. PEOPLE CHOOSE THEIR EVENTS TO CREATE THESE SYMBOLS OR PERHAPS WE SHOULD SAY THEY CREATE THE EVENT WITH THE UNCONSCIOUS KNOWLEDGE THAT IT HAS AN APPROPRIATE SYMBOLIC CORRESPONDENCE, WHICH IS ALWAYS A MESSAGE OR STATEMENT. WHETHER IT IS FROM A DREAM OR FROM WAKING LIFE YOU WILL ALWAYS FIND YOU CAN ISOLATE CERTAIN CHOICES YOU MADE IN ORDER TO CREATE THAT PARTICULAR EVENT. ULTIMATELY, IT IS NOT THE EVENT BUT THE CHOICE YOU MADE TO CREATE THAT EVENT. IF YOU CORRESPOND YOUR CHOICE TO THE SYMBOL RATHER THAN THE EVENT YOU WILL READ AN EVEN DEEPER MEANING INTO THE SITUATION BECAUSE BEHIND EVERY CHOICE THERE IS A MOTIVE. UNDERSTAND YOUR MOTIVES AND YOU WILL UNDERSTAND YOURSELF.

THE METAPHYSICAL LANGUAGE IS COMPRISED OF SYMBOLS. THIS IS PARTLY HOW THE DREAM MIND OPERATES. NOT ONLY ARE THESE SYMBOLS DRAWN FROM PRESENT SITUATIONS BUT FROM THE PAST AS WELL, INCLUDING PAST LIVES. HOWEVER, THERE WILL ALWAYS BE A CORRESPONDENCE TO WHAT IS PRESENTLY

GOING ON. EVEN ARCHETYPAL DREAMS THAT
REFLECT AN EXPERIENCE OF THE SOUL, DEN-
OTING THE PROGRESS OR SUM TOTAL OF
EXPERIENCES WHICH HAVE OCCURRED OVER
A PERIOD OF MANY LIVES, WILL STILL RELATE
TO THE PRESENT IN SOME FASHION.

IN ANSWER TO YOUR QUESTION ABOUT
ANIMALS, ANIMALS REFER MAINLY TO PER-
SONALITY CHARACTERISTICS. OCCASIONALLY,
AN ANIMAL WILL BE USED AS AN ARCHETYPAL
OR SPIRITUAL SYMBOL, BUT EVEN THEN IT CAN
USUALLY BE TRACED TO A PERSONALITY TRAIT.
THIS BEING THE CASE, IF YOU LOOK AT EACH
PARTICULAR ANIMAL AND DETERMINE THE
CHARACTERISTICS OF THAT ANIMAL, YOU
WILL FIND THE KEY TO ITS SYMBOLIC MEAN-
ING. A SNAKE FOR INSTANCE, HAS TO DO
PARTICULARLY WITH FEARS. THIS IS BECAUSE
ALMOST EVERYONE HAS BEEN BITTEN BY A
SNAKE IN ONE INCARNATION OR ANOTHER. IT
MAY DEPICT A VENOMOUS ASPECT OR INDIVID-
UAL SUCH AS A *SNAKE IN THE GRASS*. ALSO,
IT CAN SYMBOLIZE SEX OR TEMPTATION.
BECAUSE IT INVOLVES THE LOWEST CHAKRA,
IT HAS A DIRECT CORRESPONDENCE TO THE
KUNDALINI, WHICH IS THE TRUE SYMBOL OF
THE BIBLICAL SNAKE IN THE GARDEN OF EDEN.
IN THIS MANNER AN ANIMAL SYMBOL MAY BE
AMPLIFIED TO ITS DEEPER MEANING. BUT
BECAUSE THESE SYMBOLS ARE LITTLE UNDER-
STOOD BY THE HUMAN RACE AT LARGE, THE
FOCUS IS MORE ON THE MUNDANE LEVEL THAN
THE ESOTERIC, EVEN THOUGH THERE IS A
RELATIONSHIP. THIS HOLDS TRUE WITH ALL
SYMBOLS; YOU WILL HAVE BOTH AN ESOTERIC

AND EXOTERIC MEANING AND ONE LEVEL WILL ALWAYS BE STRONGER THAN THE OTHER IN A DREAM.

Snakes are a fairly common symbol in dreams. Here is a snake dream submitted by a student.

> *I was in mom's bedroom sitting on her bed and wanting to arrange a meeting with my teacher Paul. I call and try to arrange a meeting but I'm told it can't be done. I'm given the number of another place to call but the line is busy. Now my mother is sitting on the bed with me holding her pet snake. It's huge, an ugly blue-gray color with cold, blue, dead looking eyes. Mom says it's angry and appears as frightened of it as I am. It starts to make striking motions and I rush off the bed, leaving my schoolbooks behind. I grab two pillows and run out of the room.*

Paul was this woman's mentor in her M.A. program and she was indeed having a communication problem with him. Therefore, the situation was literal. Delving deeper into the dream, we found it also revolved around her feelings about school and the project she had undertaken. Paul now becomes symbolic of an issue over her schooling and the problem she has relating to it. The first part of the dream illustrates the problem, the second part illustrates the source of the problem. We have all heard the expression: *It's your bed, you lie in it.* In this case it was her mother's bed, which consisted of certain values and expectations that the dreamer chose to accept by *sitting on her mother's bed.* She felt both fearful and threatened by her mother's perfectionist attitude regarding her academic performance.

Examining her own feelings about school, she discovered a measure of insecurity over living up to the standards imposed upon her. Wishing to escape the situation she runs off, leaving her schoolbooks behind and taking two pillows. Sleep is often a form of escape, which is why she took the pillows. Working with this dream caused her to see that she had transferred her mother's feelings onto herself and it was undermining her scholastic endeavors. By getting in touch with her inner feelings she resolved the situation by redefining her goals, affirming self-acceptance and releasing her perfectionist attitude toward her studies.

TOPDOG/UNDERDOG

We commonly accept another's feelings, attitudes and points of view as our own, especially our parents'. We incorporate them into our own thinking, accepting them at face value and believing that such ideas and opinions are ours. But because we didn't reach these conclusions ourselves, they always remain outside influences, commonly portrayed in our dreams by the very figures we allowed to program or otherwise influence us. If they assume an internal authority role as in the above dream, they are known as *topdogs*. The dreamer then assumes the role of *underdog*. These terms were coined by Fritz Perls, and a dialogue technique employing these two characters is now extensively used in gestalt therapy.[6] Widely publicized by Ann Faraday in her book *The Dream Game*, she states the topdog defines the internal authority attempting to impose its will upon the personality, and the resistant counterpart *underdog*, who wants to have everything its own way.[7] Many disturbing and nightmare type dreams arise from topdog-underdog conflicts. Incorporated into our lives by those whose authority has influenced us, they trigger a childlike reaction, setting into motion dreams such as the previous example.

"Are topdogs generally characteristic of the feelings that others have projected onto us?" I once asked.

NO, THEY ARE REFLECTIONS OF YOUR OWN LEARNING AND ABILITY TO PROJECT. YOU DO NOT MANIFEST ANYTHING IN YOUR DREAM LIFE THAT IS NOT YOUR OWN, A PART OF YOUR PERSONA OR EGO. THE TOPDOG IS AN INTERNAL MECHANISM OF PROJECTING ONTO THE SELF WHAT *SHOULD* BE DONE. OTHERWISE, YOU WOULD FIND IN EVERYONE THAT THEY WOULD BE ABSORBING EACH OTHER'S EXPECTATIONS. *SHOULD* IS A WORD THAT THE HUMAN RACE WOULD BE BETTER OFF WITHOUT.

INSECTS AND FISH

Besides people and animals, insects and fish are also common symbols in dreams. The following two dreams are my own. One concerns insects, and the other fish. I asked my dream guides for help, and their interpretations follow.

My cat's tail was full of bugs and I had to cut it off. All this time my phone was ringing.

THIS DREAM IS TELLING YOU THAT YOU MUST CUT SOMETHING OFF THAT IS BUGGING YOU, SOMETHING THAT IS FOLLOWING OR *TAILING* YOU. THE PHONE RINGING IN THE BACKGROUND TELLS YOU WHAT IT IS. IT IS THE CONSTANT DEMAND OF OTHERS FOR YOUR TIME AND ATTENTION.

I'm looking into my aquarium and see it's full of baby fish that are either dead or dying.

THE AQUARIUM IS YOUR MIND AND THE FISH ARE PLANS OR IDEAS THAT YOU HAD. THE FACT

THAT THEY WERE BABIES INDICATES THAT THEY WERE STILL IN THE DEVELOPMENTAL STAGE. THE DREAM IS TELLING YOU THAT THE IDEAS WHICH YOU HAVE BEEN NURTURING ARE ALMOST DEAD. INSECTS WILL USUALLY MEAN ANNOYANCES AND FISH WILL BE EITHER THOUGHTS OR DESIRES, WHATEVER IS SWIMMING AROUND IN YOUR MIND. AN AQUARIUM IS A TANK SYMBOLIZING A THINK TANK. REMEMBER, ONLY HALF THE SYMBOL IS TO BE FOUND IN THE CHARACTER, THE OTHER HALF IS FOUND IN WHAT THE CHARACTER IS DOING.

Fish represent desires when we dream of fishing. Attempting to catch a fish means we are fishing for something—a client, a job, a raise or even a mate. Catching a fish usually means we have succeeded in *landing* what we sought.

NUMBERS

Perhaps the most difficult symbol to interpret is numbers. Often, I've had to wrestle with trying to figure out their meaning. Finally I devoted an entire session to this subject, asking my guides to explain the use of numbers and how to interpret them.

NUMBERS ARE USED TO EXPLAIN AN ABSTRACTION. ONE ABSTRACTION IS TIME. IT CAN BE THE TIME SOMETHING IS HAPPENING OR WILL HAPPEN, AN ARRIVAL OR DEPARTURE, A TIME PERIOD SUCH AS A TIME IN A PERSON'S LIFE, OR A PAST TIME OR MOMENT. ABSTRACT SYMBOLS SUCH AS NUMBERS ARE USED TO CONDENSE A RATHER COMPLEX IDEA INTO A SIMPLE RENDERING THAT WILL FIT INTO A

DREAM. FOR EXAMPLE, A PERSON MAY DREAM OF A CHILD ONE-AND-A-HALF YEARS OLD. LIKE ALL SYMBOLS IT IS A CONDENSATION. IT COULD REFER TO A TYPE OF BEHAVIOR THAT WILL HAVE RAMIFICATIONS FOR ONE-AND-A-HALF YEARS, OR A TYPE OF BEHAVIOR THAT OCCURRED AT AGE ONE-AND-A-HALF. IT COULD ALSO MEAN A TYPE OF BEHAVIOR THAT HAS BEEN GOING ON FOR ONE-AND-A-HALF YEARS. IT BRINGS THE CHARACTER OF THE PERSON INTO CONTEXT BY SUPPLYING IT WITH AN AGE.

THE BEST WAY TO RESOLVE NUMBERS IS TO ANALYZE THE DREAM AS COMPLETELY AS POSSIBLE FIRST. THEN GO BACK AND LOOK AT THE DREAM. YOU MUST SEE HOW THE NUMBER FITS INTO THE GENERAL CONTEXT OF THE DREAM. REMEMBER, THE SAME NUMBER CAN HAVE DIFFERENT MEANINGS IN DIFFERENT DREAMS. IT IS NOT A CUT-AND-DRIED PROCESS. THINK OF THE NUMBER AS A CONCEPT, THEN ATTEMPT TO FIT THAT CONCEPT INTO THE DREAM. IF IT DOESN'T FIT, TRY ANOTHER. CONTINUE UNTIL YOU ARRIVE AT ONE THAT FITS THE CONTEXT OF THE DREAM CORRECTLY.

Enthusiastic with the information I was receiving, I flipped through my dream journal searching for previously earmarked pages of dreams incorporating numbers. The first that fell into this category is as follows:

I went into a newly remodeled tropical fish store and found it under different management. I recognized the new owner, who had been painting. Feeling tired, he had fallen asleep. I woke him up and he showed me around. During this time I gave him suggestions and told him I would be very happy to help him. I returned to the store later and it was like a restaurant. A family was sitting down eating and they invited me to partake. I sat down next to the owner's wife, to whom I felt particularly close. When I got up to pay the bill I remembered that I had not paid for my last meal and the bill included both meals. It totaled twenty-five dollars.

THIS DREAM IS FAIRLY LITERAL ABOUT YOUR EXPERIENCE AT WORK. YOU ARE TO HELP IN REDOING THE STORE. THE OWNER IS TIRING AND TEMPORARILY ASLEEP TO HIS ROLE IN THE STORE BECAUSE SO MUCH IS GOING ON IN HIS PERSONAL LIFE. YOU WOKE HIM UP TO HIS ENTHUSIASM WITH A CLEAR MESSAGE THAT YOU WILL BE HELPING HIM. YOU ALSO KNOW HIS WIFE FROM A PAST LIFE. THE PEOPLE AT THE TABLE ARE THOSE WHOM YOU WILL BE WORKING WITH AND ARE RELATIVE TO YOUR JOB SITUATION. THE LAST JOB YOU HAD DID NOT PAY OFF; THIS ONE WILL. CONSEQUENTLY IT WILL MAKE UP FOR THE BALANCE OWING. THE NUMBER TWENTY-FIVE VIBRATES TO A SEVEN. IT IS A VERY POWERFUL NUMBER BECAUSE IT CONTAINS FIVE FIVES. THERE IS A VERY STABLE BASE OF A STRONG VIBRATION IN FIVE AND SEVEN. IT MEANS YOU ARE COMING TO TERMS WITH YOUR LAST JOB BY WORKING THROUGH THIS ONE. IT SIGNIFIES A BINDING TOGETHER AND CONSEQUENTLY AN EXPANSION OF YOUR EXPERIENCE IN THE WORKPLACE. ALSO, IT DENOTES A COMPLETION OF CERTAIN ASPECTS OF THIS EXPERIENCE AS YOU HAVE COME TO A PEAK TIME

IN YOUR TENTH HOUSE [career] ACTIVITIES.

In the next dream I was trying to ring up some figures on an old-time cash register and kept getting wrong numbers. They were popping up higher than they should have and I had to manually push them down before I could rering them. I pushed sixteen dollars and forty cents, but the cash register showed seventy dollars.

HERE WE HAVE A TIME SYMBOL, EVEN THOUGH IT IS WITHIN THE CONTEXT OF MONEY. EIGHT IS A MONEY NUMBER AND WE HAVE TWO OF THEM IN SIXTEEN. TWO MONIES LUMPED TOGETHER OR TWO LUMPS OF MONEY INDICATE TWO PAY PERIODS, AS THAT IS WHEN YOU RECEIVE A LUMP OF MONEY. FORTY REDUCES TO FOUR, WHICH IS HALF OF EIGHT. WE NOW HAVE TWO-AND-A-HALF PAY PERIODS. YOU ARE HOPING TO RECEIVE A RAISE BY MID-JANUARY. YOUR DREAM IS SHOWING YOU THAT IT IS NOT GOING TO HAPPEN AT THIS TIME. IT WILL BE SEVENTY DAYS LONGER THAN YOU WISH. YOU WILL NOT HAVE THE RESULTS YOU ARE ANTICIPATING UNTIL THEN.

ON THE PHYSICAL PLANE MONEY PLAYS A VITAL ROLE, ESPECIALLY IN MORE AFFLUENT COUNTRIES. PEOPLE IN UNDERDEVELOPED COUNTRIES DO NOT USE THE MONEY SYMBOL AS MUCH BECAUSE IT IS NOT A FACTOR TO CONSIDER. WHEN YOU HAVE DOLLARS AND CENTS IN A DREAM, LOOK FIRST TO SEE IF THERE IS A LITERAL TRANSLATION. THEN LOOK TO SEE IF THERE IS A COST INVOLVED. ASK WHAT IS COSTING YOU IN YOUR LIFE? WHAT ARE YOU HAVING TO PAY FOR? IF YOU

FIND YOU ARE HAVING TO PAY FOR SOMETHING
THEN THE NUMBER WILL GIVE YOU AN INDI-
CATION OF THE AREA YOU ARE PAYING IN, OR
EXACTLY WHAT YOU ARE PAYING FOR, WHICH
MAY OR MAY NOT BE IN PHYSICAL DOLLARS
AND CENTS. IF YOU ARE BEING PAID SOME-
THING, THE NUMBER WILL GIVE YOU AN
INDICATION OF THINGS THAT ARE BEING GIVEN
TO YOU OR WHAT YOU HAVE RIGHTLY EARNED.
IF YOU USE THE WORDS SURROUNDING THE
NUMBER IT SHOULD HELP TO CLARIFY THE
SITUATION. ARE YOU PAYING OUT OR BEING
PAID? IS IT COSTING TOO MUCH OR TOO
LITTLE? THE NUMBER TWO, FOR EXAMPLE,
COULD REPRESENT TOO MUCH. IT COULD ALSO
SYMBOLIZE A COUPLE, A RELATIONSHIP OR
ANY OF THE ESOTERIC MEANINGS SURROUND-
ING THE NUMBER TWO.

*I dreamt I was trying to catch a big fish in the river. There
were many other fishermen around. I hooked it and it felt
very big. I played it for twenty-six minutes and when I
brought it in it only weighed out at three-and-a-half pounds.
I felt it should have weighed at least five pounds. When
someone asked why it took me so long to bring it in, I
said because I was only using four-pound test line.*

TWENTY-SIX MINUTES REFERS TO TWENTY-SIX
MONTHS. YOU FEEL THAT BY THIS TIME YOU
SHOULD BE EARNING MORE MONEY. YOU
ATTEMPT TO JUSTIFY YOUR PRESENT EARN-
INGS BY SAYING YOU DIDN'T TRY AS HARD AS
YOU COULD HAVE TO RAISE YOUR SALARY.
THAT WAS YOUR PLAYING IT OUT WITH LIGHT
TACKLE INSTEAD OF USING A MORE FORCEFUL

APPROACH. FIVE POUNDS HAS TO DO WITH THE ESOTERIC MEANING FOR THE NUMBER FIVE. FIVE WOULD BE A SUBSTANTIAL INCREASE OR *CHANGE* IN WHAT YOU PRESENTLY EARN. THREE-AND-A-HALF IS INSUFFICIENT.

"How did you get twenty-six months out of twenty-six minutes?"

YOU HAD BEEN PLAYING IT FOR TWENTY-SIX SOMETHING AND YOU KNOW IT WAS LONGER THAN TWENTY-SIX MINUTES, HOURS OR DAYS. EVEN TWENTY SIX WEEKS IS TOO SHORT AND IT OBVIOUSLY HAS NOT BEEN TWENTY-SIX YEARS. WHEN DEALING WITH TIME SPANS LOOK FIRST LITERALLY, THEN SEE IF THERE IS A POSSIBLE PRECOGNITIVE ASPECT. NOTE WHETHER WHAT HAPPENED IN THAT REFERENCE IS PRESENTLY HAPPENING OR WHETHER IT IS CONNECTED TO THE PAST OR FUTURE. IF ONE DREAMS OF HOURS IT MAY REFER TO *OURS* AS WELL AS REFERRING TO A TIME PERIOD. IF THERE IS A WAITING CONCEPT IN THE DREAM, HOURS MAY REFER TO A LONG OR SHORT PERIOD OF TIME. NUMBERS ON A CLOCK, FOR EXAMPLE, CLEARLY INDICATE A PERIOD OF TIME. THREE-FIFTEEN COULD SIGNIFY THE FIFTEENTH OF MARCH. IF ONE HAPPENS TO BE VERSED IN NAVIGATION THE TIME COULD ACTUALLY MEAN A POSITION. THIS IS TRUE EVEN FOR THOSE WHO ARE UNSCHOOLED. TWELVE NOON COULD REPRESENT A MIDPOINT, TWELVE MIDNIGHT AN ENDING. EARLY HOURS COULD SIGNIFY SOMETHING JUST BEGINNING AND LATE HOURS SOMETHING THAT IS LATE OR ENDING.

"Would you please elaborate on the significance of ages in dreams?"

AGES USUALLY REFER TO A STAGE OF DEVELOPMENT. IF YOU HAPPEN TO DREAM OF A TWENTY-TWO YEAR OLD, YOU ARE DREAMING OF SOMETHING FAIRLY SPIRITUAL OR SIGNIFICANT BECAUSE OF THE INTENSE VIBRATION OF THE NUMBER TWENTY-TWO. YOU CAN THEN LOOK FOR A STAGE OF SPIRITUAL DEVELOPMENT IN YOUR LIFE. IT CAN ALSO MEAN SOMETHING THAT YOU WERE DEALING WITH AT AGE TWENTY-TWO, OR SOMEONE ELSE THAT YOU KNOW OR KNEW WHO WAS TWENTY-TWO AT THE TIME.

"How about a count of objects, like a half dozen eggs?"

ALWAYS FIRST DETERMINE WHAT THE OBJECT MEANS. ONCE THE MEANING IS CLEAR THEN THE NUMBER CAN FIT IN, EITHER IN REFERENCE TO A QUALITY THAT THE OBJECT HAS, OR A PERIOD OF TIME THAT THE OBJECT REFERS TO OR RELATES WITH. IN GENERAL THERE ARE THREE LEVELS TO CHECK WHEN ATTEMPTING TO DECIPHER THE MEANING OF NUMBERS: FIRST, THE QUALITY OF THE NUMBER ON A SYMBOLIC OR ESOTERIC LEVEL; SECONDLY, THE PARTICULAR STATE OF DEVELOPMENT THAT OCCURS AT THAT TIME IN TERMS OF YEARS; LASTLY, THE LITERAL INTERPRETATION SUCH AS THE TIME ON THE CLOCK, DATE ON THE CALENDAR, ET CETERA.

"What about a given number of people? Like the dream I had with thirteen thousand people."

THIS WILL ALMOST ALWAYS REFER TO A CHARACTER. YOU CORRECTLY INTERPRETED THIS DREAM AS HAVING TRANSFORMATIONAL QUALITIES. THE NUMBER THIRTEEN IS TRANSFORMATION. YOU HAVE ADDED THOUSAND AFTER IT, MAKING IT A STRONG OR POWERFUL TRANSFORMATION. ZEROS AFTER A NUMBER USUALLY MAGNIFY THE SYMBOL. OFTEN, WHEN YOU DREAM OF A SPECIFIC NUMBER OF PEOPLE YOU WILL FIND AN ESOTERIC OR INHERENT QUALITY TO THAT NUMBER.

"I've had dreams where there was no reference given to the number. Why is that?"

WHEN A NUMBER OCCURS WITHOUT REFERENCE TO A PARTICULAR OBJECT, SUCH AS THE NUMBER FLASHING BEFORE YOUR EYES, OR SEEN ON A BILLBOARD, BLACKBOARD, MARQUEE OR EVEN A HANDWRITTEN NOTE, YOU MUST PAY PARTICULAR ATTENTION TO THE WHOLE DREAM. ANALYZE IT AS SOMETHING SURROUNDING THE NUMBER. KEEP THE WORD *SIGN* FOREMOST IN YOUR MIND WHILE YOU ARE ANALYZING. THE NUMBER IS A SIGN FOR YOU AND WILL ALMOST ALWAYS HAVE AN ESOTERIC MEANING.

COLORS

"Is the symbolism of colors the same as numbers in that it's not beyond the average person's ability to comprehend?

In other words, color symbolism isn't deeply esoteric unless the dreamer is familiar with the esoteric meanings. Am I correct?"

NO, BECAUSE ON INNER LEVELS THE DREAMER MAY BE PERFECTLY AWARE OF THESE DEEPER MEANINGS. OUTWARDLY HOWEVER, THEY MAY HAVE A DIFFICULT TIME UNDERSTANDING SUCH DREAMS. IT COULD BE THAT THEY ARE PROMPTING THE OUTER EGO OR THE PERSONALITY TO WAKE UP TO THE DEEPER LEVELS OF AWARENESS. THERE IS ALSO THE FACT OF DUAL SYMBOLISM, ONE HAVING A MUNDANE MEANING WHILE THE OTHER HAS A MUCH DEEPER ONE. LOOK AT THE DIFFERENCES HERE BETWEEN COLORS AND NUMBERS. COLOR IS NOT AT ALL IN THE SAME REALM AS NUMBERS. COLORS BELONG TO THE ASTRAL REALM WHILE NUMBERS ARE OF THE MENTAL. COLORS HAVE TO DO MORE WITH FEELINGS OR EMOTIONS WHILE NUMBERS ARE GOVERNED BY THE LAWS THAT APPLY TO THE MENTAL PLANE. THE VIBRATIONS OF COLOR CAN INFLUENCE THE MIND, BUT ONLY THROUGH THE ASTRAL BODY, THAT IS, WITH THE EXCEPTION OF WHITE.

"In the handouts for the dream class, I outlined the different colors and what they represented. I feel the definitions are rather sketchy and need further elaboration. How should I go about this?"

YOU SIMPLY TAKE AN ATTRIBUTE OF THE COLOR AND DEMONSTRATE THE ATTRIBUTE, SEEING HOW IT CAN BE TURNED NEGATIVELY

AND POSITIVELY. RED FOR EXAMPLE, IS STRONG, VITAL ENERGY. ITS POSITIVE ATTRI-BUTE WOULD BE ENTHUSIASM, PHYSICAL VIGOR AND SO FORTH. ON THE NEGATIVE END IT WOULD BE PHYSICAL FRUSTRATION, EXCES-SIVE ENERGY, ANGER, ET CETERA. YOU CAN MOVE RIGHT DOWN THE LINE WITH THE COLORS, STARTING AT A NEUTRAL SPOT AND SWINGING FROM POSITIVE TO NEGATIVE. THIS WILL SHOW THAT ALTHOUGH ONE COLOR CAN HAVE MANY DIVERSE MEANINGS THEY ARE ALL LOGICALLY CONNECTED AND IT IS NOT THAT HARD TO FIGURE OUT.

3

The Structure of Dreams

Besides examining the dream content, we should also note its presentation or how the dream is laid out. Sometimes dreams begin with an introduction encapsulating the theme about to be presented—something like a preview. I once began a dream by viewing a four-story building. Interestingly enough, it contained four seemingly separate stories revolving around a single issue. Another time, the dream began with me riding a bicycle. Later, I unraveled a message pointing to *two* issues in my life in need of *balance*. I always pay particular attention to the first sentence of the dream; it usually outlines the theme or plot. The following randomly selected examples will hopefully serve to illustrate my point.

I'm in a waiting room.

This is telling the dreamer that she is waiting for something. The main body of the dream reveals what it is. A room that we occupy is the *space* that we're in. She was in a *waiting space*.

I'm watching a movie about two kids fighting.

The movie is a presentation of the drama. It deals

either with a personality clash or an inner conflict, resulting in immature behavior.

I'm walking down the street nude.

Nudity is revealing or exposing something about oneself, usually one's feelings: "the naked truth" or "bare facts." In this case it reflects a direction the dreamer is taking.

Weird plants are growing in my back yard.

This initial sentence is saying there are some strange thoughts growing in the back of the dreamer's mind. Plants are what we cultivate and the back yard is symbolic of the subconscious or unconscious.

I'm going to the bathroom.

Going to the bathroom is a process of elimination. It reveals the dreamer as eliminating something from his or her life. Urinating is eliminating a yin characteristic and a bowel movement represents eliminating a yang trait or feeling.

Someone is pointing out an island to me.

Here we have the dream pointing something out. An island is a solitary or isolated aspect. Something is being isolated and pointed out to the dreamer.

As we can now see, the first sentence of a dream often suggests what the dream is about. The last sentence can also be equally revealing. Sometimes it is offering advice, but most often it is showing us a position we have taken, a conclusion we have reached or an effect we caused.

There are no hard-and-fast rules to dream structure. I cannot say that the first sentence will always be as revealing as the examples I have shown, nor the endings always offer advice or a summation. They are merely areas to check when deciphering a dream.

SHIFTS

One area that gave me considerable trouble concerned dreams that shifted from one theme or plot to another. It was like having two or more dreams contained in one. I would be doing something in one scene, when suddenly I am transported elsewhere, finding myself doing something entirely different. Determined to ask for an explanation for these occurrences, I took several dreams containing what I call *shifts*, and brought them to our next channeling session.

"What is the significance and function of shifts in dreams?" I asked.

YOU HAVE BROUGHT SOME EXAMPLES WITH YOU. LET US BEGIN WITH THOSE.

I was riding with a friend into a fun tunnel at some sort of arcade. The car was on a conveyor and there was a large spider on the wall which appeared quite real, but which I recognized as fake.

SHIFT

Now I'm at a house meeting some ladies. We are going to a party. I remember being in the house and feeling at home there. It felt familiar, like a place I had been to before, a long time ago.

THIS IS A GOOD EXAMPLE OF HOW SHIFTS ARE USED. HERE, YOU SHIFT FROM THE GENERAL TO THE SPECIFIC. THE BEGINNING OF THE DREAM IS A GENERAL STATEMENT THAT SOME FUN IS TAKING PLACE, AND SOME FEARS REGARDING THE OPPOSITE SEX ARE RECOGNIZED AS NOT THREATENING OR AS UNFOUNDED. THE DREAM NOW SHIFTS TO THE

SPECIFIC WHERE YOU COME INTO CONTACT WITH INDIVIDUALS OF THE OPPOSITE SEX, WHICH IS EXPERIENCED AS FUN. WHAT IS IMPORTANT TO UNDERSTAND IS THAT THE FIRST PART BASICALLY SAID: *HERE IS YOUR MESSAGE,* **AND THE SECOND PART SAID:** *IT HAS TO DO WITH THIS.*

Recalling the experience that triggered the dream, I saw it stemmed from a recent occurrence when I felt pressured into a double date by a friend of mine. In the dream I vaguely remember the car we were riding in connected to other cars, symbolizing that a connection was being made. Spiders can represent the dark side of females and I must admit, after my last relationship I was quite wary. Yet, it turned to be a real *fun* experience, and I wound up thoroughly enjoying myself and my companion, a familiar feeling I had not *housed* in a long time.

The next dream example belongs to a dream student:

I was on my way home and I leaned too far forward while walking, losing my footing in a shallow ditch. I did a flip and landed on my feet. This happened again later. I reached the house and noticed the trees had fall leaves with many beautiful colors. These were somehow connected to me doing flips and made me feel wonderful.

SHIFT

Now I'm inside my house with a group of other people. We were having a buffet and Denise was upset about something. I remember we talked for a long time.

IN THE FIRST PART OF THIS DREAM CERTAIN SHALLOW ASPECTS OF THE PERSONALITY ARE BEING WORKED OUT. EVEN THOUGH THESE ARE WEAKNESSES, SHE IS LANDING ON HER

FEET. THE FALL LEAVES ARE INDICATIVE OF THE FALL SEASON WHICH WE ARE NOW IN. SHE CONTINUES TO LAND ON HER FEET WHILE COMING INTO THIS PARTICULAR PERIOD, THE FALL. WE SEE A SERIES OF STUMBLES LEADING TO A VERY POSITIVE PERIOD, WHICH IS WHY SHE FEELS SO WONDERFUL. THEN, SHE IS BACK HOME. THERE IS A BUFFET, DENISE IS UPSET, THEY TALK, ET CETERA. HERE WE HAVE A SHIFT SAYING: *MEANWHILE, BACK AT THE RANCH OF EXPERIENCE, THIS IS WHAT IS GOING ON*. WE NOW HAVE A DIFFERENT USE OF THE SHIFT TO SWITCH FROM ONE TIME PERIOD TO ANOTHER, FROM ONE FOCUS OR PERSPECTIVE TO ANOTHER. THE DREAM WILL USE SHIFTS WHEN IT ATTEMPTS TO EXPLAIN MANY DIFFERENT THINGS INCLUDING TIME PERIODS SIMULTANEOUSLY.

I submitted another dream for interpretation from the same student.

I was in a storeroom at work and I had this mouse that I released. Then I saw Santa Claus. He had a gold decoration around his neck. As I wondered at what I saw, the floor gave way to scintillating lights of different colors . . . like stars blinking. I felt the giving spirit, the heart of the meaning of Santa in a very profound way.

SHIFT

Now I'm at home with my parents and the rest of my family, telling them I won't be there for Christmas.

THIS DREAM PERTAINS TO RELEASING HER TIMIDITY BY TELLING HER PARENTS THAT SHE CHOSE NOT TO SPEND CHRISTMAS WITH THEM,

EVEN THOUGH IT IS A FAMILY TRADITION. A FURTHER AWARENESS WAS BROUGHT TO MIND AS A RESULT OF RELEASING THE MOUSE, SO TO SPEAK. IT HAD TO DO WITH THE SYMBOLISM OF THE SANTA AND CHRISTMAS, WHICH WAS SO ELOQUENTLY DESCRIBED IN THE DREAM. THEN IT SHIFTS TO THE HOME AND FAMILY AND A CERTAIN AMOUNT OF HOLLOWNESS ASSOCIATED WITH IT. THE FIRST PART OF THE DREAM EXPLAINS A LESSON THAT HAS BEEN LEARNED. THE SECOND PART DEALS WITH HOW IT CAN BE APPLIED. OVER AND OVER YOU WILL FIND A PATTERN IN SHIFTS, BRINGING A PERSON FROM A GENERAL TO A SPECIFIC, FROM AN EXPLANATION TO AN APPLICATION, FROM A BROAD TIME PERIOD TO A SPECIFIC TIME PERIOD, FROM THE FUTURE OR PAST TO THE PRESENT. THE SHIFT'S PURPOSE IS TO BRING THE ATTENTION OF THE DREAMER FROM THE CAUSE, THE GENERAL, THE OUTLINE OR ACTION, TO THE RESULT, THE SPECIFIC, THE CONSEQUENCE OR RAMIFICATION. THERE WILL ALWAYS BE A *FROM* SHIFT *TO*. YOU STUDY WHAT IT IS COMING FROM AND WHAT IT IS GOING TO. SOON YOU WILL ARRIVE AT THE GENERAL CATEGORIES THAT SHIFTS ARE USED IN.

"Sometimes a dream changes and yet it's not exactly a shift. Can you explain the difference?"

IN DREAMS THAT CHANGE SCENES AND DO NOT ACTUALLY SHIFT, THERE IS NO *FROM-TO* RELATIONSHIP. THIS IS USUALLY UNDERSTOOD BY THE DREAMER WITHOUT HAVING TO CON-

SCIOUSLY MAKE A DISTINCTION BETWEEN THE TWO. A CHANGE HAS TO DO WITH DIFFERENT ASPECTS OF THE SAME ISSUE, AS THOUGH YOU ARE SEEING DIFFERENT POINTS OF VIEW WITHIN THE SAME FRAME OF REFERENCE. A SHIFT ENCOMPASSES DIFFERENT REFERENCES AND ASPECTS OF THE SAME OR DIFFERENT ISSUES WHICH HAVE A CAUSE AND EFFECT RELATIONSHIP.

THEME AND PLOT

Dream composition usually contains both a theme and a plot. A theme is the direction or mood of the dream. Was it happy, light, friendly and warm? Was it frightening, disturbing, sad or dark? The theme revolves around an activity, usually the plot. A good approach to understanding your dreams is to follow the theme into the plot. The plot is the main issue of the dream. A theme is like a melody and a plot the arrangement of the notes. If you dream you are swimming in a river and nothing else, the theme could be "immersion." Look at the setting: is it day or night? The answer could reveal whether it was a conscious or unconscious activity. What was the rest of the setting like? Peaceful and enjoyable? The fact that you were alone may possibly signify a solitary performance. When you ask yourself what activity you were performing you arrive at the plot: *swimming.* Assuming this was the entire dream, the plot or main issue is swimming, which has you *singly* or *solely immersed* in something. A river could represent the flow of your life. The dream would then be telling you that you are immersed in an activity that adds to the flow of your life, or an activity that has you caught up in its current, etc. Inactivity, can mean something you are not doing and that would be part of the theme. A more dramatic theme is found in a dream I recently had:

There is a tremendous implosion and I see a section of a city sucked into a large pit in the ground, carrying many people including myself downward. I crawl out and although obviously injured, I feel no pain. People see me and turn away. I feel blood is oozing out from my eyes.

The mood was one of shock coupled with amazement. If we follow the activity, we see I fell into something caused not by an upheaval but an *inheaval.* When I came out, I was not in the same condition as when I fell in, suggesting a theme of transformation. The plot has me suddenly falling into the earth and emerging again, indicating an inner transformation took place which didn't leave me unscathed. For those who are curious, here is what my guides had to say about this dream:

IN MANY CASES, BLOOD IS ASSOCIATED WITH THE KUNDALINI WHICH YOU ARE WORKING WITH . . . THE VITAL ENERGY AND LIFE FORCE. THIS SOMETIMES IS ALSO THE CASE WITH MENSTRUAL BLOOD WHICH, WITHIN THE DREAM STATE, REFERS TO THE KUNDALINI ENERGY. THERE IS SOMEWHAT OF AN IMBAL-ANCE OF THIS ENERGY WITHIN YOURSELF AT THIS TIME, AS THE KUNDALINI IS AWAKENING AND BUILDING TO A CONSIDERABLE EXTENT. THERE IS A GREAT DEAL OF ENERGY THAT IS AFFECTING YOU INWARDLY AS IT WOULD BE OPENING UP WITH INCREASING FORCE. WHAT IS BEING SEEN IS THAT THIS ENERGY, GROWING AND OPENING WITHIN YOU, IS HAVING A DISRUPTIVE EFFECT ON THAT OF THE NERVOUS SYSTEM AND EMOTIONS, AS IT WOULD BE OPENING AT A TREMENDOUS RATE. THE PART

OF THE DREAM WHERE BLOOD WAS COMING OUT OF YOUR EYES SHOWS THE ENERGY YOU PROJECT WOULD BE FELT BY OTHERS, AND MAY BE INTIMIDATING TO THEM AT CERTAIN TIMES. THERE IS A NEED TO CHANNEL THIS ENERGY BY GOING INTO A MEDITATIVE STATE AND PULLING IT UP USING THAT OF THE TANTRIC BREATH . . .

The message continued by giving me some exercises to aid in the balancing of these energies.[1] The point I wish to make, however, is that considerable headway can be made in interpreting a dream by examining both the theme and plot. Besides the plot, we also have subplots, areas of related importance to the main body of the dream. The dream has a body or main message and the subplot is an issue of related importance that fits in. A *sidewalk* is sometimes a symbol of a *side issue* since it runs parallel to the street or thoroughfare of the dream.

DREAM LEVELS

We now know there are always two sides to a dream, the esoteric and the exoteric. One is always stronger than the other. The above dream was definitely esoteric. The exoteric interpretation would be inner emotional upheavals of a transforming quality. We can also view the experience as occurring on two different levels, the emotional and the spiritual. In the previous chapter I attempted to show how a dream could be amplified to higher levels. All dreams are multilevel, corresponding to levels the dreamer is operating on. If, for instance, we have a dream dealing with something taking place on the physical level but with emotional undercurrents, we then have two levels we can immediately discern.

My "blood" dream clearly manifested as an emotional level dream. Upon reflection, I noticed my frustration level was higher, my patience less, and I tended to become somewhat more reclusive. Under more stressful circumstances, it was quite possible I could have become ill, thus affecting my physical condition. Had this been the case I'm sure the dream would have focused more on the physical. If it reached the point where this disturbance affected my judgment then it would have included the mental level as well. Occasionally we have characters portraying or symbolizing these different states. One character will portray what is happening in the dreamer's physical life, another will act out what is transpiring on a mental level, while another depicts the dreamer's emotional response. A different character can symbolize each level, or we can have a single character representing a multiple of these levels.

Dreams can be assigned to four basic levels:

1. *The literal or physical level.*
2. *The emotional or feeling level.*
3. *The mental or idea level.*
4. *The spiritual or archetypal level.*

Although the dream may manifest upon all these levels simultaneously, one level will usually be predominant. I would classify my blood dream as a level two dream since it described the emotional effect these energies were having upon me. It was the level I needed to work on most. A level one dream would focus more on physical or material issues. The following is an interesting example of a level one dream:

A nun wearing red tights over her black garments asked me how much I would charge to paint her nunnery. I surveyed the large building and estimated it would take many gallons of white paint. I figured the cost out to be around two thousand dollars.

At this time, I found myself financially overextended. I did not know the exact sum and was resisting tallying it up. Nun was a play on words for *none*. The tights meant *tight money*, while red over black stated I was in the *red* instead of being in the black. The large building or nunnery housed the *debts* that I built up. The gallons of paint represented the *labor* it would take to clean up this debt, which turned out to be very close to *two thousand dollars.*.

Once, as I was preparing dinner, I overcooked the broccoli. I wondered if I really lost as many nutrients as they claim by overcooking vegetables. It was a fleeting thought that crossed my mind and vanished in a split second, yet resulted in the following dream:

> *I'm a laborer picking broccoli at a farm. I pull up some fresh broccoli from underneath a layer of snow, and place it in the back of my pickup truck. I see a patch where the snow has melted and the broccoli is in the direct sun. Some are partially dry-looking and I don't pick them. Now it becomes overcast and starts to snow. We stop and the farm owner sees a truck with a refrigerator in back. He tells the driver that it's a "Golden Harvest" appliance and he collects them.*

I felt the dream was telling me the less cooked the broccoli is, the better. And since heat destroys the nutrients—they preferably should be eaten raw. On another level, it could be I am reaping what I have sown, some positive and some not so positive. A change in the weather could signify a change in myself would assure me of a golden harvest. Weather can be symbolic of temperament, mood or emotion. I suggest that dreamworkers attempt to pull from as many levels as possible when working with their dreams. This was a level one dream, concerning dietary advice, but with possible level four overtones. It's also interesting that a fleeting thought, forgotten almost as quickly as it passed, can implant itself in our subconscious like a seed, from which emerges a dream.

The dream concerning dead and dying baby fish in the last chapter was a level three dream as could be the hypothetical swimming dream discussed earlier. Most dreams are reflective of what is on the dreamer's mind, and often occur when we are grappling with a problem. Sometimes they are more mental, particularly with students or those working with figures or equations. Level four dreams, which are purely archetypal or spiritual, are not as common. I feel this is because many of our dreams already share this level even though it may not be obvious. In looking over dozens of my dreams that I felt were predominantly spiritual, I found them to be rather unimpressive. What cannot be conveyed in words is the profound feelings they produce. I noticed this to be true with examples from other dreamers as well. To the best of my knowledge, a level four dream is always uplifting and encouraging. Often, they are psychic or astral dreams where we have contact with our higher selves and our spiritual guides or teachers.

Another factor to consider when examining the dream structure is its relative complexity. We have already learned that the vagueness, simplicity or complexity of a dream reveals our present state of awareness:

1. A vague or difficult-to-remember dream relates to either an undeveloped ability for dream recall or a disinterest in what is transpiring on inner levels.

2. A complex dream is usually very long. If it is principally mundane, with little symbolic content, then the dreamer is primarily projecting him or herself into the outer world. This suggests inner confusion over preoccupation with outer concerns. If the symbolic content is high, it means the dreamer is grappling with deeper inner impulses, which as yet are not sufficiently integrated.

3. The simple dream is usually short with deep symbolic

content. Generally reflective of a clearer state of consciousness, it is attained by those familiar with dreamwork, or those who have in some way consciously worked on clearing themselves.

RECURRING DREAMS

Another question we may ask ourselves is if we have had a dream with a similar theme. Specific dream themes recur in our lives with each turn of the spiral. They form a pattern known as repeating or recurring dreams, dealing with the same topic each time they come around. In seeking to learn more about such dreams, I asked my guides for further elaboration.

SUCH DREAMS INDICATE THAT AN ISSUE IS AGAIN AT HAND AND IS BEING DEALT WITH ON A HIGHER LEVEL. THIS IS A HEALTHY PATTERN. SINCE THE MOVEMENT OF TIME IS NOT LINEAL BUT SPIRAL, WE HAVE REPEATING CYCLES OF GROWTH. BETWEEN EACH SPAN IS A DEVELOP-MENTAL PERIOD WHERE THE INDIVIDUAL ASSIMILATES THE EXPERIENCE AND PRO-GRESSES. NOW THE SAME ISSUE WILL COME AROUND ON THE NEXT TURN OF THE SPIRAL REGARDLESS OF WHETHER THERE HAS BEEN ANY PROGRESS. IF THE INDIVIDUAL HAS NOT PROGRESSED VERY FAR, THE PROBLEM WILL NOT BE MET ON A HIGHER LEVEL, BUT ON THE SAME LEVEL AS BEFORE. IF THE PERSON CONTINUES TO MEET THE SAME PROBLEM ON THE SAME LEVEL WITHOUT ANY SIGNIFICANT ADVANCEMENT, THE CONDITION WILL DETERI-ORATE. THEN YOU WILL FIND A DEGENERATION INTO INCREASINGLY SEVERE FORMS OF NIGHT-MARES. HOWEVER, THE SAME OCCURRENCE

OF PATTERNS DOES NOT NECESSARILY HAVE TO RESULT IN A NIGHTMARE. INDEED, YOU MAY SEE IT PROGRESS TO A DREAM WHERE THE NIGHTMARISH SYMBOLS ARE USED BUT ARE NO LONGER FEARFUL. SUCH DREAMS ARE CON-SIDERED MAJOR BECAUSE THEY REFER TO LARGE LIFE PATTERNS OR LESSONS BEING WORKED OUT.

USUALLY, THESE MORE SIGNIFICANT THEMES WILL BE ADDRESSED OVER PERIODS OF YEARS, IF NOT INCARNATIONS. THIS WOULD BE CON-SIDERED A LONG-TERM PATTERN. IN A SHORT-TERM PATTERN, YOU WILL FIND THAT WHEN AN ISSUE IS BEING DEALT WITH, THE SAME PATTERN OF MESSAGES AND THE SAME TYPE OF SYMBOLS WILL BE USED IN A STEADY STREAM OVER AND OVER AGAIN. THIS WILL CONTINUE UNTIL THE LESSON IS WORKED THROUGH ON INNER LEVELS TO AN EXTENT THAT THE SOUL FEELS IS SUFFICIENT. THESE DREAMS WILL THEN CEASE FOR A TIME BEFORE STARTING UP AGAIN. THE PURPOSE OF THESE PATTERNS—NO MATTER WHAT TIME SPAN THEY COVER, LONG OR SHORT—IS TO AGAIN BRING TO THE ATTENTION OF THE DREAMER THE PARTICULAR MESSAGE AND NOTE THE PROGRESS BEING MADE IN THAT AREA.

4

Types of Dreams

NIGHTMARES

Calvin Hall writes in his book *The Meaning of Dreams* that a nightmare is produced when one is at odds with one's conscience.[1] A punishment dream for some misdeed, it is considered a negative experience generally reflective of deep levels of fear and anxiety. In her book *The Dream Game*, Ann Faraday isolates two major nightmare producing culprits. One is the Topdog:

> "A 'self-punishment' nightmare occurs whenever underdog has defied topdog during the day, in which case topdog hounds him again at night in order to regain control over him. On the other hand, when topdog has denied underdog a really basic need during the day, underdog, driven to the end of his tether, comes out in a thoroughly nasty way at night. In either case, it is a fight to the death, which accounts for the feeling of dread and terror in the nightmare itself."[2]

The other, she claims, is Jung's infamous archetypal figure *The Shadow*. The concept of the Shadow is that it reflects the "dark side" of us. It is a nasty, inferior, corrupt and worthless part of ourselves, which is in direct contrast to our pleasant and charming persona. The Shadow is limited to the same sex as the dreamer because Jung felt the dreamer is more compassionate of the opposite sex. This figure, associated with one's lower or base instincts, is an aspect which by its very nature cannot be shown compassion. Therefore, Jung reasoned it must always appear as the same sex, assuming a negative role that we might consciously disown, but which nonetheless exists within our psyche.

Essentially, Dr. Faraday traced her nightmare figures to be "either conscience in search of retribution, or the Shadow in search of acceptance."[3] A nightmare can be triggered whenever we go against our feelings, sometimes associated with breaking some sort of "rule" imposed upon us during the formative years of childhood. For the most part, psychology is in agreement that a nightmare is the voice of our conscience, trumpeting our fears, guilts or conflicts. The problem remaining is how best to deal or otherwise resolve these inner feelings that cause such nightly distress.

We have an element within the dream field that believes in confronting and making peace with your dream adversaries. They feel this somehow helps the dreamer to integrate or resolve the issue. I believe this may tend to relieve the emotional impact of the nightmare, defusing it in one way or another, but does little to address the underlying cause. My feeling is that you can only resolve your conflicts in the dream state to the extent they are resolved in your waking life. Dreams are a reflection that cannot be changed without first changing the image that produces that reflection. You may cheat on your mate, steal from your employer and beat your kids, but you will never accept and make peace with that part of yourself without first eliminating it from your life. Then and only then can amends be made.

There are of course more "honorable" issues that can produce fertile grounds for a nightmare, such as the high expectations we place upon ourselves, our criticalness and our restrictive moral attitudes—all of which restrain and imprison us in a world of our own making. My advice is to confront your adversary and ask for the issue to be pointed out clearly, so that you may deal with it in the waking state. By pinpointing particular areas where we are struggling or having conflicts, we may then discover the cause.

There are degrees of anxiety, and while nightmares express our deepest fears we also have less frightening types of unpleasant dreams. They are what I call disturbing dreams. Once, when in a position of authority, it was my unpleasant duty to dismiss a subordinate. That night, I dreamed I was beheaded by execution. Underlining the word *I* and the word depicting what I was doing which was being *beheaded,* tells me I am beheading someone. I quickly understood that by *executing* an order I gave someone *the ax.* It was a disturbing experience having to fire this man, and was mirrored in my dream.

This could also be labeled a violent dream. Such dreams do not necessarily reflect a violent nature. In fact, even the most timid and peace loving are not immune from this type of dream. Violent dreams most often occur when we are struggling with a conflict, combating an illness or dealing with our fears.

The most destructive attribute we must deal with is fear. It robs us of our peace of mind, destroys our sense of security, cheats us out of our self-confidence and erodes our health. It is important to realize that on some level we must always face our fears. There is no other way to overcome them. Because fear is so unbalancing, it must ultimately surface in our dreams. Another type of anxiety dream is one based upon unfounded fears. These I call groundless fear dreams. Unfortunately, such dreams are often mistaken as precognitive, thus escalating our fears even further. My wife had a series of dreams prior to our wedding of an empty church, or empty tables at our reception. As it turned out, she couldn't have been more wrong. The church was filled to capacity and I had to break away from the reception line to have someone set up more tables. Often, I come across groundless fear dreams of people catching sexual diseases, losing their jobs, their families and even their lives. Such dreams are simply reflecting what is on the dreamer's mind. A point to remember is precognitive dreams usually occur only once, while fear dreams are repetitive, or so I am told.

A GOOD THING TO ASK WHEN YOU HAVE A FEARFUL SITUATION IN A DREAM IS NOT ONLY WHAT YOU FEAR IN THE USUAL SENSE, BUT WHAT YOU DON'T WANT TO SEE OR HEAR. NORMALLY, WE DON'T THINK OF SUCH ISSUES IN A MANNER OF ACTUALLY BEING AFRAID OF THEM, BUT THAT IS EXACTLY WHAT IT IS. BY TURNING YOUR BACK TO IT IN WAKING LIFE, YOU ARE TURNING TO FACE IT IN YOUR DREAM LIFE.

Kate, a woman acquaintance, once told me of a recurring dream where she was in a spooky old house climbing up a creaky staircase. The house was rather dark, and she was extremely afraid of what awaited her at the top. The farther up she climbed, the greater her fear became, until she suddenly awoke, never quite making it to the top. Having had this dream since childhood, she was curious to know what it meant. After taking it up with my teachers, I found it had to do with religious matters. It was a parental topdog dream, dealing with a fear impressed upon her in childhood. At a very young age she was told that if she was bad she would be punished in the afterlife. Whenever she felt she didn't measure up to her religion's standards for *being good*, she would trigger this dream.

Guilt is a powerful nightmare inducer and is the product of our own judgmentalness. We make mistakes so that we may learn from them. That is our main purpose for being here. Guilt serves no function other than to make us miserable.

Unfortunately, it is not so easily detected. In fact, most people would deny its existence within themselves, at least until they became proficient at interpreting their dreams or employing some other method of analysis. Essentially, fearful dreams should be looked upon as an excellent opportunity to help pinpoint a conflict or negative issue, enabling us to confront and eradicate an unhealthy condition from our lives.

HEALTH DREAMS

Health dreams are far more prevalent than we realize. They are constantly guiding and giving us feedback on our physical condition. Pregnant women are especially prone to such dreams, not only during the duration of their pregnancy, but for some time thereafter. The following dream is from a newly pregnant student:

Leaving a cafeteria with a cup of black tea, I slip past the register without paying. I spill some on my white shorts, staining them. Then I meet a friend who in waking life just had a baby. She tells me she's pregnant.

This dreamer drank some coffee that day and had trouble falling asleep later. Not much of a coffee drinker, she occasionally would have a cup of black tea. I don't know if the dream was pointing to the staining substance in tea (tannic acid), or whether caffeine was the problem. Whatever the case, she can't get away *without paying,* even though she's trying.

Usually there is a certain amount of concern during pregnancy. This opens the door to fearful dreams. Dreams of the baby dying in the womb or born deformed are not uncommon. Again, remember that frightening or disturbing dreams are often simply reflections of our own fears. They are something we must come face to face with in the dream state. Normally, most health-related pregnancy dreams are presented in such a manner as to alert us without undue alarm. One exception however, is near the end of the pregnancy when the mother-to-be dreams of the infant's death. This signifies the *death* or *ending* of the pregnancy.

William A. McGarey, M.D., tells the following story in his book *The Edgar Cayce Remedies,* about a patient of his who suffered from aches and pains in his joints.

> I heard a knock at the door, and it was a kindly looking old man who nodded to me, entered the house without being invited, and motioned for me to follow him. He took me downstairs to the cellar, showed me the drain pipes to the bathrooms in the house, and told me they were all plugged up and would let hardly any water through. That was the end of the dream.[4]

Dr. McGarey states: "It did not take the knowledge of a genius to interpret the dream as a sign that the eliminations of the body were in poor shape, and that they should be corrected, if the man was to have a healthy body once more. The communication from the unconscious realm to the conscious awareness comes most often in complicated symbols, but the messages are always there for those who will look at the dream content and try to understand."

I believe we never encounter an illness without being forewarned in a dream. Such a dream often outlines the mental or emotional conditions that initially instigated the illness. Once a student submitted a dream where she was in a war, bitterly fighting opposing forces. I told her the dream was a warning that she was fighting off an illness and to look after it. Three weeks later she came down with the flu, which she described as "The worst in my life." Often having such dreams myself, I usually end up fighting Nazis, since they represent bad GERMans. One of my faults is that I don't drink enough liquids. A few health dreams I asked for help with, are as follows:

A huge sea creature was stranded upon a beach. It had propeller-like fins which were barely turning, indicating it was quite weak.

IT SIGNIFIES A NEED FOR MORE LIQUID IN THE BODY. THE LARGENESS OF THE CREATURE SUGGESTS THE VAST AMOUNT OF FLUID NEEDED.

I see a friend of mine in a wading pool with alfalfa sprouts and water. Then I shoot a water gun out of which came more sprouts.

YOU NEED MORE MINERALS AND LIQUIDS, THAT'S ALL.

A werewolf is rapidly bounding downhill toward me. I turn and begin to run. As I look back over my shoulder it's almost upon me.

YOUR HEALTH IS RAPIDLY GOING DOWNHILL AND ILLNESS WILL BESET YOU IN APPROXI-MATELY THREE DAYS, ABOUT THE TIME OF THE FULL MOON. DRINKING LOTS OF MINT TEA WITH FRESH LEMON JUICE WILL HELP TO ALKALIZE YOUR SYSTEM AND KILL THE BAC-TERIA THAT ARE PRESENT.

I took my guide's advice and it worked. I didn't catch the cold or flu that was beginning to form. I also swore off werewolf movies.

In one of my dreams, I was a passenger on an airplane. Looking out the window, I saw we were over Korea. Since I had no conscious connection with that country, I couldn't decipher the dream's meaning. I set it aside, intending to present it at our next channeling session, but I didn't have to wait that long. A few days later, I kept a doctor's appointment to determine what was wrong with my hearing, as I could barely hear out of one ear. The examination showed an accumulation of ear wax had built up, which was easily removed. The dream was my first experience (that I know of) with an anagram, where the letters when rearranged a different way form a name or message. Here, the dream was telling me that my EAR was OK.

Another area I suffer with is my teeth. Having had gum surgery, I now must practice greater oral hygiene to prevent future problems. The following dreams revolve around this issue:

I'm with my dentist, who is also a personal friend of mine. In the dream he shows me the controls to a boat he used to have. I said they looked just like mine. He is living on this boat, which I recognize as mine. I ask him what he is doing there, and I notice my ship-to-shore radio is missing. I become upset and demand an explanation.

The dream is telling me that I'm not controlling my oral hygiene as instructed. A lack of communication, evidenced by the missing radio, means I'm not heeding my dentist's advice and find I owe myself an explanation. I asked for help with this next dream:

Lying on an operating table, my dentist is about to perform a hernia operation on me (I actually had one about three months previously). He said the operation would take six to eight hours.

A PRECOGNITIVE DREAM TELLING YOU WILL HAVE SOME ORAL SURGERY ON TWO OF YOUR

TEETH IN SIX TO EIGHT MONTHS.

"How did you get two teeth from the dream?" I asked.

THE WORD *TO*, SANDWICHED BETWEEN SIX AND EIGHT MEANS *TWO*. ALSO, THE DIFFERENCE BETWEEN SIX AND EIGHT IS TWO.

Discovering there were two teeth causing problems, I redoubled my efforts, giving them considerable attention. That was nine months ago as of this writing, and I still have them. Both are wisdom teeth however, and feeling it is not worth the effort, I am planning to have them removed.

Dreams also point to our attitudes as causative factors regarding illnesses. Modern science is now beginning to support this fact. In *Science of the Mind,* Ernest Holmes gives many correspondences.[6] A few are llustrated here:

Tumors: *Destructive emotions and desires, eating away at oneself.*

Constipation: *Fear, restriction, inactivity, limitation.*

Heart Trouble: *Problems of the love nature, hard heartedness.*

Hardening of the Arteries: *Stubbornness, narrow mindedness. (All blood circulation problems can be traced to restrictive or inflexible thought.)*

Colds: *More colds result from damp spirits than from wet feet.*

Deafness: *Refusal to hear or listen.*

Vision: *Refusal to see things clearly and properly.*

Rheumatism: *Evasion of responsibility, failure to act.*

Arthritis: *Again, regarding movement. Not lifting a finger when both hands and arms are needed, or not standing up for yourself or others when required.*

Stomach Problems: *Worry, distrust, anxiety.*

High Blood Pressure: *Failure to keep peace of mind, anger, emotional excitement.*

Kidneys: *worry, anxiety, fear and criticism.*

Edgar Cayce once stated:

> "To be sure, the attitudes oft influence the physical condition of the body. No one can hate his neighbor and not have stomach or liver trouble. One cannot be jealous and allow anger of same, and not have upset digestion or heart disorder." (4021-1)[5]

We can now see how thought as well as diet can profoundly affect our health. Worry, anger and fear are the greatest perpetrators of ill health. It's also a known fact that stress ages and weakens us, while a positive frame of mind keeps us young and vital. In many respects we are living symbols. When sabotaging ourselves either through illness or accidents, we often choose a part of the body that will in some way make a statement by having a symbolic corresspondence. Be alert for dream messages concerning your health. They can do much to help prevent or lessen an oncoming illness.

HYPNAGOGIC

While not considered to be a dream state per se, it does play an important role warranting consideration. I felt this state merely reflected the day's events and our own thoughts, possibly subconsciously reviewing and evaluating material to determine just what is relevant to us on an inner level. When I questioned my guides about it, I received this interesting reply:

YOU WILL FIND A SIMILARITY HERE TO WHAT AN INFANT EXPERIENCES—SOMETIMES EVEN IN THE WAKING STATE. THIS PARTICULAR EXPERIENCE IS CARRIED FROM BIRTH. ESSEN-

TIALLY IT IS A FREEING OF THE MIND, AN ABILITY TO BE STILL WITHIN THE BODY, AND UNHOOK ONESELF FROM THE CONCRETE MENTAL LEVEL. THIS IMMEDIATELY EXPANDS THE CONSCIOUSNESS TO A POINT WHERE IT CAN TAP INTO THE SYMBOLIC REALM. IT IS A PECULIAR COMBINATION OF THE DREAM AND WAKING STATES. AN INFANT HAS NOT FORMED A STRONG MIND AND DOES NOT HAVE A SET MENTAL PERCEPTION OF THINGS. IT EXPE-RIENCES ITS OWN SYMBOLIC WORLD OR LAN-GUAGE ALL THE TIME. AS WE GROW, WE EXPERIENCE THIS LESS AND LESS UNTIL IT IS CONFINED TO JUST BEFORE FALLING ASLEEP. HOWEVER, YOU WILL FIND THAT IF YOU DEEPLY RELAX WITH YOUR EYES STILL OPEN, YOU WILL BEGIN TO SEE THINGS. THIS IS A TRUE DAYDREAM. ALL IT REQUIRES IS AN UNHOOK-ING OF THE MIND. YOU CAN INDUCE A HYP-NAGOGIC STATE AT WILL IF YOU DO THIS, AND IMMEDIATELY FIND AN EXPANSION AND INFLOW FROM THE SYMBOLIC WORLD.

"But these symbols are random, unimportant fragments of things, with no continuity or meaning," I countered.

WHEN YOU HAVE AN EXPERIENCE, THE MIND WILL IMMEDIATELY PUT IT IN ORDER, PLACE IT IN A PERSPECTIVE AND COMPARE OR RELATE IT TO ANOTHER EXPERIENCE. NOW, WITHOUT THE MENTAL INPUT, THE EXPERIENCE IS SIMPLY ASSIMILATED ON A SYMBOLIC LEVEL AND YOU SEE THE SYMBOLS FLOATING BY, SO TO SPEAK. THEY DON'T HAVE ANY CONTINU-ITY BECAUSE THE MIND IS NOT THERE TO PUT

THEM IN ORDER BY CATEGORIZING AND ORDERING A SEQUENTIAL FLOW. THIS IS WHAT THE MENTAL IS USED FOR. IT PUTS THE SYMBOLS IN ORDER, BUT THAT DOES NOT MEAN THE SYMBOLS HAVE NO MEANING WITHOUT AN ORDERLY ARRANGEMENT. IT IS SIMPLY THAT THE HUMAN MIND CANNOT UNDERSTAND THEM WITHOUT ORDER, AT LEAST NOT IN ITS PRESENT STAGE OF EVOLUTION.

"There are a couple of experiences I had in the hypnagogic state. Once, when I was taking a bath and deeply relaxed, I had a vision of my tooth crumbling. A few days later, this actually happened. Was this precognitive?"

IT WOULD SEEM TO YOU THAT HAVING A VISION OF A TOOTH CRUMBLING WAS RANDOM AND HAD NO MEANING. THIS IS BECAUSE YOUR CONCRETE MIND COULD NOT PUT IT IN ORDER. ONCE IT TRULY HAPPENED, YOU HAD SOMETHING WITH WHICH TO RELATE. THE MIND IS FAIRLY LIMITED IN THE RESPECT THAT IT CAN ONLY DRAW UPON THE PAST. IN THIS INSTANCE YOU PULLED IT FROM OUTSIDE THE CONTEXT OF TIME.

"The other experience involved seeing a Chinese man by the name of Dow who was reading the newspaper. Earlier in the day I had been looking at the Dow-Jones listings of gold prices in the newspaper. Why would I have a vision of that?"

FIRST, YOU ARE FOCUSING ON THE WORD INSTEAD OF THE CHARACTER. WHILE SOMETIMES THIS IS HELPFUL, THE FACT IS, YOU

USED A CHINESE MAN. THIS MAKES IT MORE SIGNIFICANT. WHEN YOU TAKE THAT INTO CONSIDERATION AND COUPLE IT WITH THE FACT THAT YOU USED A CHINESE WORD LIKE *TAO*, YOU HAVE MUCH MORE OF A SPIRITUAL MEANING. DREAMS ARE NOT ORDERED IN A MANNER THE MIND CAN READILY GRASP. YOU ARE THE ONE WHO HAS OFTEN SAID A DREAM DOES NOT ALWAYS FLOW IN SEQUENCE OR ORDER.

ABSTRACT DREAMS

What I term abstract dreams are those which consist of forms, patterns and colorful symbols, usually not associated with feelings. I had been unable to make any sense out of such dreams, and felt that perhaps they denote some form of communication with the superconscious or soul. Again, taking this question to my ethereal teachers, I asked:

"Do abstract dreams come from a mental level?"

OCCASIONALLY, ESPECIALLY WHEN YOU ARE COMMUNICATING WITH YOUR TEACHER ON THAT LEVEL. THE ABSTRACT MENTAL PLANE IS USUALLY WHERE YOU COMMUNICATE WITH YOUR HIGHER SELF AND OTHER EVOLVED BEINGS. YOU MUST THINK OF THE MENTAL PLANE AS HAVING TWO LEVELS, THE ABSTRACT AND THE CONCRETE. YOU MAY EXPERIENCE DREAMS FROM EITHER LEVEL.

"There were times when doing a lot of studying I would dream about numbers, formulas, equations and geometric symbols. Isn't that considered abstract?"

THIS IS MORE ON THE CONCRETE MENTAL LEVEL, SIMILAR TO WHEN YOU USE A TAPE IN SLEEP LEARNING. WHAT IT DOES IS SYNTHES-IZE THE ENERGIES OF THE HIGHER MENTAL OR EVEN PERHAPS THE SUBCONSCIOUS WITH YOUR CONCRETE MENTAL. WHEN THIS IS INTEGRATED TO THE EXTENT THAT THE CON-CRETE MIND BECOMES MORE OF A TOOL THAT DIRECTLY PERCEIVES, IT IS MORE EFFECTIVE. IF YOU ARE LEARNING IN AN OPEN-MINDED AND RELAXED STATE, YOU ARE DRAWING ON THE HIGHER ASPECTS OF THE MIND. THIS IS WHAT HAPPENS WHEN YOU ARE SLEEPING OR DREAMING. YOU ARE IN FACT LEARNING WITH HIGHER ASPECTS OF THE MENTAL PLANE AND THIS FILTERS DOWN INTO THE CONCRETE MENTAL, SO BOTH ARE INVOLVED AT THE SAME TIME. NOW, WHEN YOU HAVE A TRUE AB-STRACT DREAM THE CONCRETE MIND IS NOT INVOLVED. THIS IS BECAUSE IT WAS NOT INITIATED FROM THE CONCRETE MENTAL LEVEL. CONCRETE DREAMS HAVE TO DO WITH THOSE THINGS THAT ARE NEEDED TO BE UNDERSTOOD ON THAT LEVEL. ABSTRACT DREAMS ARE ALMOST UNIVERSALLY SPIRIT-UALLY ORIENTED.

WISH-FULFILLMENT

Unable to find any suitable examples, I began to wonder about the term "wish fulfillment" as described by Freud.[7] *In Working With Dreams,* by Montague Ullman M.D. and Nan Zimmerman, the question was raised, "Are dreams wish-fulfilling?" to which the authors responded:

"Wish-fulfillment is certainly an aspect of dreams but, in my opinion, is by no means their sole instigator. I don't think there is any one need that shapes a dream. I think that dreaming is a naturally recurring period of partial arousal during sleep, which occurs when our brain is awake enough to give us the opportunity to react to any tension arising out of our recent life experience."[8]

Curious, I asked my dream guides if there indeed was such a thing as a wish-fulfillment dream, and if so, how does it work?

NOT REALLY. IT IS A GRAVE MISCONCEPTION WHICH SERVES TO SIDETRACK PSYCHOLOGISTS AND PREVENTS THEM FROM SEEING THE TRUE ISSUE OF THE DREAM. IT IS MUCH TOO SIMPLE A LABEL FOR A THING AS COMPLEX AS A DREAM. IF A PERSON IS EXPERIENCING THE FULFILLMENT OF A WISH IN A DREAM, THAT IS USUALLY NOT THE KEY ISSUE. HOW IS THE PERSON FEELING IN THE DREAM AND HOW ARE THEY GOING ABOUT FULFILLING IT? WHO ARE THE DIFFERENT CHARACTERS AND WHAT DO THEY REPRESENT? WHAT DOES THE WISH ITSELF SYMBOLIZE? A PERSON DOES NOT DREAM ABOUT SOMETHING THAT IS OB-VIOUSLY SO CONSCIOUS. THERE HAS TO BE SOME UNDERLYING OR DEEPER MEANING TO THE WISH TO HAVE IT SURFACE IN A DREAM. A STRONG WISH HAS TO DO WITH THE DESIRE NATURE, AND IT USUALLY REVOLVES AROUND SOMETHING MATERIAL. THIS, THEN BECOMES SYMBOLIC OF A DEEPER INNER NEED.

FOR EXAMPLE, YOU WILL FIND ELIZABETH AT ONE POINT DREAMING CONSIDERABLY OF SEXUAL RELATIONSHIPS WITH OTHER WOMEN.

THIS COULD PERHAPS, BE SHALLOWLY INTER-
PRETED AS WISH FULFILLMENT SINCE THOSE
WERE HER DESIRES AT THE TIME, BUT UNDER-
NEATH YOU WILL FIND A MORE IMPORTANT
THEME OF INSECURITY VERSUS SECURITY. A
NEED FOR INNER FULFILLMENT AND FOR
CERTAIN INTEGRATIONS TO TRANSPIRE. EACH
OF HER DREAMS WILL HAVE A DIFFERENT
INTERPRETATION; SOMETIMES THEY WILL
MEAN INTEGRATION AND SOMETIMES THEY
WILL MEAN JUST THE OPPOSITE, SUCH AS A
LONGING FOR INTEGRATION THAT IS NOT
TAKING PLACE. TO BRAND OR LABEL A DREAM
AS MERELY WISH FULFILLMENT IS TO SIMPLIFY
THE DREAM MESSAGE TO A POINT WHERE IT
HAS NO MEANING.

SOMATIC DREAMS

Dream studies have shown that outside stimuli can affect
our dreaming. An ice cube placed on a dreamer can cause
him or her to dream of an arctic climate, while an overly
warm dry room can stimulate a desert experience. Other
physically related events also take place as we dream, and
I was curious to see what kind of information I could get
on this subject.

"How do somatic dreams work?" was my first question.

A DREAM IS FORMED IN THE MIND, WHICH IS
NOT IN THE BODY PER SE. IT IS THEN SENT TO
THE BRAIN IN MUCH THE SAME MANNER AS
YOUR COMPUTER SENDS ITS MESSAGE TO THE
PRINTER—FIRST TO THE BRAIN, THEN ON TO
THE NERVOUS SYSTEM. A SOMATIC DREAM

WORKS IN THE REVERSE. FIRST THE NERVOUS SYSTEM IS STIMULATED, THEN THE BRAIN, WHICH AFFECTS THE MIND.

"What about talking in your sleep and sleepwalking? Are they sometimes related to emotional disturbances of the individual?"

NO, ALTHOUGH SOME PEOPLE DEMONSTRATE A STRONGER CONNECTION WITH THEIR EMOTIONAL THAN OTHERS, AND IT IS POSSIBLE TO PERMEATE THEIR PHYSICAL BODY WHILE STILL IN THE DREAM STATE, SUCH A RESPONSE COMES FROM A HEIGHTENED OR INTENSE EMOTIONAL BODY. THERE CAN BE A DESIRE ON THE PART OF THE DREAMER TO MOVE IN ORDER TO BE MORE COMFORTABLE, AND THIS CAN OCCUR WITHOUT DISTURBING THE DREAM STATE. ONE CAN ALSO WALK ABOUT WITHOUT DISTURBING THEIR DREAMS. SLEEPWALKERS TEND TO EXHIBIT A STRONGER EMOTIONAL BODY THAN NORMAL, BUT IT DOES NOT MEAN THEY ARE EMOTIONALLY DISTURBED. IN SOME CASES, THE PHYSICAL BODY IS SIMPLY FOLLOWING THE ACTIVITIES OF ITS ASTRAL COUNTERPART. TALKING IN ONE'S SLEEP IS LESS CONNECTED TO THE EMOTIONAL. IT HAS TO DO WITH THE ASTRAL BODY BEING IN VERY CLOSE TOUCH WITH THE PHYSICAL, AND A BLEED-THROUGH EFFECT OCCURS.

"What is the link between rapid eye movement and dreaming?"

AS WE HAVE SAID EARLIER, DREAMING OCCURS

IN THE MIND AND THERE IS A VERY STRONG
STIMULATION TO THE BRAIN. HUMAN SIGHT IS
ESSENTIALLY A REACTION TO NERVOUS
IMPULSE AND THE SAME KINDS OF NERVOUS
IMPULSES ARE TRANSMITTED IN THE DREAM
STATE. DREAMING DOES NOT TAKE PLACE
WHILE YOU ARE OUT OF YOUR BODY, IT
HAPPENS IN THE MIND WHICH STIMULATES
THE BRAIN. IN TURN, THE BRAIN STIMULATES
THE NERVES TO THE EYES.

Sounds can also induce dreams. I remember dreaming of seeing a foot-long mosquito before awakening to the high pitched hum of a mosquito flying around me. The exaggerated size probably meant my chances of getting bit were large. Another time I dreamt of piloting my truck underwater, like a submarine. That day, I left the truck parked outside by my bedroom. During the night it rained quite heavily. A spout angled from the roof gutter poured rain water through my open truck window. The next morning, six inches of water rushed out to greet me when I opened the cab door. My subconscious evidently knew what was taking place and created a little dream to warn me.

THE SENOI

I originally read about the Senoi in Charles Tart's *Altered States of Consciousness.*[9] Frequently mentioned in dream texts, their concepts have now found a permanent niche in the annals of dreamwork. The Senoi are a peaceful tribe of Malaysian indians whose culture revolves to a great extent around dreams. Every morning family members would traditionally discuss their dreams with one another. One of the things they attempt to do in their dreams is actively change the dream from within. If they encounter something threatening in a dream they either challenge it or attempt to make peace with it, depending upon the circumstances. When dreaming of making love, they always strive to complete the experience, inevitably attempting to receive a gift from the character or figure within the dream.

The Senoi, who for the most part have been swallowed up by civilization, were first reported in *Dream Theory in Malaya*, a paper submitted many years ago by Kilton Stewart, an American psychologist working in conjunction with Herbert Noone, a British anthropologist. The most recent published work concerning contact with the Senoi is recorded by Patricia Garfield in her book *Creative Dreaming*. Dr. Garfield flew to the Malay peninsula to conduct a personal study of these people, interviewing tribal members through an interpreter, who translated their aboriginal language into Malay and then into English.[10]

Her report makes a convincing argument, stating that applying the "Senoi system of dream control" will help unify or otherwise integrate the personality. She further attests that negative dream images are transformed into positive ones, or at least into those no longer frightening. The latter I can understand, but I had difficulty believing that a dream could do all the work for us in terms of our evolutionary growth, which is in effect what integration is all about. Curious as to what the teachers had to say, I asked for some feedback:

PEOPLE CANNOT BRING THEMSELVES TO DO SOMETHING IN THEIR DREAM LIFE UNTIL THEY HAVE REACHED A POINT WHERE THEY CAN DO IT IN THEIR WAKING STATE. IT CANNOT BE APPROACHED FROM BOTH DIRECTIONS. WHEN YOU RESOLVE SOMETHING IN THE WAKING STATE YOUR DREAMS WILL REFLECT THAT, POSSIBLY BY RECONCILIATION OR A SPONTANE-OUS TURNING TO MEET THE ENEMY. THIS OCCURS WITHOUT ANY ATTEMPT TO CONTROL

THE DREAM LIFE. FROM THE OTHER END, YOU MAY WORK AS DILIGENTLY AS YOU WISH AND WILL NOT BE ABLE TO TURN AND MEET YOUR OPPRESSOR, AT LEAST NOT UNTIL YOU HAVE DEVELOPED THE ABILITY TO DO SO ON THE PHYSICAL LEVEL. CONSCIOUSLY MANIPULATING THE DREAM DOES HEIGHTEN ASTRAL AWARENESS, MORE SO THAN NORMAL DREAMWORK, BUT AS FAR AS WORKING ON YOURSELF AND UNDERSTANDING DREAM MEANINGS AND SYMBOLS, IT IS OF LITTLE VALUE.

THE SENOI DID NOT SEE THEIR ATTACKERS AS SOMETHING TO INTEGRATE WITHIN THEMSELVES, NOR DID THEY ANALYZE THEIR DREAMS IN TERMS OF BEING SYMBOLIC. THEY LIVED THEIR DREAM LIKE IT WAS—A SEPARATE LIFE. THEIR WAY OF WORKING OUT WHAT THE FIGURES MEANT WAS TO WORK OUT THE DRAMA IN THEIR MINDS AND DREAM LIFE, INSTEAD OF WORKING IT OUT IN WAKING LIFE. THEIR PEACEFUL NATURE DID NOT EVOLVE FROM THEIR DREAMWORK, AS SOME MAY INSINUATE. AT SOME TIME THEY WILL HAVE TO ARRIVE AT A POINT WITHIN THEIR CONSCIOUS AWARENESS OF THE HIGHER MEANING OF SYMBOLS. IN REALITY, WHAT THEY HAD WAS A VERY SOPHISTICATED ABILITY TO WORK WITH DREAMS WITHIN A PRIMITIVE CULTURE, AN ASTRALLY ORIENTED RATHER THAN A MENTALLY ORIENTED APPROACH.

THE ASKING OF GIFTS WOULD BE SYMBOLIC OF THE ESSENCE OF THE DREAM EXPERIENCE. THIS IS BECAUSE THE GIFT OF A DREAM IS ITS MEANING, WHICH ALWAYS RELATES TO SELF-UNDERSTANDING. IT IS AN EXTERNALIZED

SYMBOL OF THE GIFT OF THE DREAM ITSELF. THROUGH THE DREAMLIFE ONE RECEIVES INSIGHT INTO ONE'S RELATIONSHIPS, INSIGHT INTO ONESELF, CREATIVE INSPIRATION AND SO ON. THE GIFTS THEY RECEIVE ARE AP-PROPRIATE TO THEIR LEVEL OF AWARENESS AND THEIR ABILITY TO UTILIZE THEM. HERE IS FOUND MUCH DREAM MEANING IN A MORE PRIMITIVE PEOPLE, WHICH GIVES THEM SOME-THING TO ACT OUT IN A PHYSICAL WAY—LIKE IN THEIR ART, SONGS, DANCE AND PROJECTS OF NATURE. WE DO NOT FEEL THIS IS OF MUCH BENEFIT TO MORE ADVANCED CULTURES WHO HAVE ALREADY SURPASSED THIS STAGE IN THEIR EVOLUTION.

LUCID DREAMING

Lucid dreaming is an area that has been receiving wide attention lately. Much work is presently being undertaken in this field. LaBerge, Keltzer, Sparrow and others have all written excellent books on the subject. According to Federik van Eeden (the first to call public attention to this type of dream), lucidity is the knowledge that one is dreaming while within the dream state. "This knowledge is accompanied by a shift in consciousness that resembles waking, although the environment is perceived as something other than the ordinary waking state."[11] Besides lucid dreaming, we also have *dream witnessing,* where the dreamer is aware he or she is dreaming, but does not have a dream body. They simply witness the dream as it unfolds.

In lucid dreaming we recognize we are dreaming. It is possible from this point to manipulate the dream if one so desires. While changing or altering a dream may provide some interesting experimentation, it may also alter what the dream is trying to explain or point out. I think it would be of greater benefit simply to observe what is going on in the dream—looking at the symbolic content and possibly trying to decipher it—while still in the dream state. Lucid dreaming is a valuable tool in that there is a much higher degree of recall than is the case with the ordinary dream. It is also possible within this state to question the dream characters. I have had only minimal experience with this type of dream. Once, while in the midst of a group of people, I suddenly discovered I was dreaming. Turning to a woman standing next to me, I asked her what this all symbolized. Her reply was, "You should know, you're the dream expert." I consider lucid dreaming as something that can be developed, although not without effort. Those involved in this type of work maintain that one's skill does improve with practice.

In my early twenties I had what I thought was a lucid dream (as it is called today). In my dream, I was walking in the Pacific Heights neighborhood of San Francisco, where as a child I had a paper route. Enjoying a magnificent view of the bay, I abruptly realized I was dreaming. Looking closely at everything, I marveled at how crystal clear it all was. I then noticed a woman about my own age or perhaps a little younger approaching. As she began walking past I grabbed her by the wrist and said "Do you know this is all a dream?" She looked startled and tried to pull away. I then grabbed her other wrist, surprised by both her response and how real she felt in my grasp. She was now terrified and struggling to escape. I felt something was wrong, this was my dream and I didn't write it to happen this way. In an attempt to calm her down, I said while still holding on to her, "Look, I'll prove it to you." and began to shake my head vigorously from side to side. I awoke still shaking my head.

Only recently did my guides confirm my suspicions that this was an astral event and not a dream. In fact, this experience disturbed me so much that I did not have another out-of-body experience for years. I would advise anyone working with lucidity in their dreams to make certain they are not having an astral experience. One of the methods for astral projection is first to become lucid in the dream state and use that as a steppingstone for leaving the body. Just as the lack of symbolism distinguishes an astral dream from an astral event, it is also used to separate a lucid dream from an out-of-body experience. If it is to be considered a dream, it must contain some symbolic content.

Autosuggestion by itself does not seem to be enough to induce lucid dreaming. One method is to bring yourself into a thoroughly relaxed state as you lie in bed, using a particular relaxation method or tape. Then replay the day's events in your mind, forgiving those who may have upset you and asking for forgiveness from those to whom you were insensitive. Affirm that you will do better with each opportunity that presents itself. This *clearing* is to alleviate many dreams that would otherwise be waiting to point all this out to you.

Make suggestions that your mind will alert your consciousness when you begin to dream so that you will be aware you are dreaming. After repeating your suggestion for at least one full minute, wait for the hypnagogic state to begin. When it does, allow yourself to remain in this half-awake state. If you focus too strongly you will wake up, and if you do not pay enough attention you will fall asleep. After a time, the hypnagogic state will abruptly cease and you will be in a state similar to a trance state. The length of time spent in this state may vary, and it is important at this point not to worry about losing sleep. That thought will signal the subconscious mind to cancel out any previous programming and quickly send you into your normal sleep pattern. At some point you will find yourself in a dream or out of your body.

A dreamer can become lucid at any point within the dream. Employing a triggering or signaling method to bring full conscious attention into the dream also helps. Suggest before you fall sleep that you stare at your hands in the dream, thus triggering awareness. Touching objects or even vocalizing (within the dream) that you are dreaming is helpful. Once you establish lucidity, it must be maintained, and this can also prove difficult. Just as in the hypnagogic state, you must maintain a dual level of awareness: one as the dream body experiencing the dream, the other as the aware body who is conscious of the fact that it is a dream. Focus too strongly on one and you have lost the other. You will either lose your awareness and continue to dream in the usual manner or you will wake up.

SEXUAL DREAMS

After awakening one morning from a highly erotic dream I decided to examine that area further. I began by soliciting material from my dream study groups, and after reaching my own conclusions, I queried my teachers.

"Can you elaborate on sexual or erotic dreams?" I asked.

AN ATTRACTIVE WOMAN IS AN ATTRACTION FOR YOU. CONSEQUENTLY, WHAT YOU ARE ATTRACTED TO IN YOUR WAKING LIFE IS OFTEN PORTRAYED IN YOUR DREAMS AS AN ATTRAC-TIVE WOMAN. IF IT IS SOMETHING APPEALING OR TEMPTING, SHE WILL APPEAR AS SEDUC-TIVE AND BECKONING. IF IT IS SOMETHING YOU PLAN TO DO OR HAVE ALREADY DONE, THEN YOU MAY EXPERIENCE SEXUAL INTERCOURSE IN THE DREAM, AS IT IS AN INTEGRATIVE SYMBOL. IF, HOWEVER, YOU ARE MERELY TOYING OR FLIRTING WITH AN IDEA IT WILL APPEAR AS SEXUAL FOREPLAY WITHOUT INTERCOURSE, PERHAPS JUST KISSING. THE

DEGREE OF PASSION EXHIBITED IN WAKING LIFE TOWARD A PARTICULAR THOUGHT, IDEA OR DESIRE IS ACCURATELY REFLECTED IN A DREAM AND GIVEN SEXUAL OVERTONES, EVEN THOUGH IT MAY HAVE ABSOLUTELY NOTHING TO DO WITH SEX. REMEMBER, AN EROTIC MIND WILL PRODUCE EROTIC DREAMS.

"What about astral sex?"

DO YOU SPEAK OF THE DREAM OR THE EVENT? IN EITHER CASE IT STILL REMAINS THE SAME— AN ATTRACTION. THE ASTRAL PLANE IS THE DESIRE PLANE AND THOSE WITH SEXUAL ATTRACTIONS AND ATTACHMENTS WILL BE DRAWN TO THAT PARTICULAR ASTRAL SUB-PLANE IN ORDER TO FULFILL THEIR DESIRES.

"Please explain the difference between the dream and the event."

FIRST, YOU HAVE A SEXUAL ENCOUNTER WITH SOMEONE ON THAT PLANE IN AN OUT-OF-BODY EXPERIENCE. IF YOU AWAKEN SOON AFTER-WARD, YOUR MEMORY OF THE ENCOUNTER WILL BE QUITE CLEAR. THIS IS THE EVENT. SOMETIMES THE EVENT CAN BE VAGUELY RECALLED LATER, BUT IT WILL ALWAYS BE STRAIGHTFORWARD, WITH LITTLE, IF ANY, SYMBOLISM. SINCE A DREAM REFLECTS AN EXPERIENCE OF THE DREAMER REGARDLESS OF WHAT PLANE THE EXPERIENCE IS TAKING PLACE, ONE MAY *DREAM* OF AN ASTRAL OCCURRENCE. THE DREAM, IF YOU HAVE ONE, WILL SYMBOLICALLY PORTRAY THE EVENT,

JUST AS WOULD ANY OTHER DREAM. IT WOULD INCLUDE YOUR THOUGHTS, FEELINGS, RESULTS AND ANY POSSIBLE RAMIFICATIONS. SINCE THESE ARE REFLECTED ON MANY LEVELS, IT MAKES A DREAM MORE COMPLEX THAN THE ASTRAL EXPERIENCE.

"What is the meaning for sexual intercourse besides integration?"

THERE IS NONE. WHAT YOU ARE DREAMING OF IS EITHER INTEGRATIVE OR REFLECTIVE OF AN ACTUAL EXPERIENCE WHICH IS ALSO INTEGRATIVE. HOWEVER, WE CAN HELP TO CLARIFY THE POINT ON INTEGRATION HERE. THE REASON ONE WOULD DREAM OF SEXUAL INTERCOURSE IN TERMS OF ONE ASPECT INTEGRATING WITH ANOTHER HAS TO DO WITH THE NEED AND DESIRE OF THE INDIVIDUAL. WATCH FOR A STRONG NEED, EMOTION OR DESIRE INVOLVED WITH THE ISSUE AT HAND, TO WHICH THE INTEGRATION BELONGS.

"Do you mean a need comparable to a sexual need?"

IN INTENSITY YES, BUT IT CAN ALSO BE A STRONG EMOTIONAL BONDING-TYPE NEED WHERE THE LACK OF INTEGRATION HAS CREATED AN EMOTIONAL VOID OR IMBALANCE IN THE FORM OF A YEARNING, PROJECTED BY FEELINGS OF EMPTINESS OR LACK. INTEGRATION SYMBOLS OF A LESS DESIROUS NATURE WILL NOT APPEAR AS SEXUAL INTERCOURSE. AN INTEGRATION SYMBOL MAY CONSIST OF ENTERING A HOUSE, CONVERSING WITH

**ANOTHER PERSON OR PUTTING ON A RING, BUT
AS SOON AS SEXUALITY ENTERS THE PICTURE
IT IS BROUGHT INTO THE REALM OF STRONG
DESIRE. SO YOU SEE, FREUD WAS NOT AS
INCORRECT AS YOU SEEM TO THINK. HIS ONLY
ERROR WAS IN NOT SEEING SEX AS SYMBOLIC
OF INTEGRATION OF THE WHOLE BEING, AND
THAT SUCH DREAMS ARE NOT CAUSED BY
SEXUAL REPRESSION AS MUCH AS BY INTE-
GRATIVE REPRESSION.**

These answers supported my own conclusions, except for
Freud. I suspect it was a little jab in retaliation for an opinion
of his sexual hypothesis that I shared at our last class. Needless
to say, I have since revised my opinion. Overall, I was quite
happy to have the rest of my conclusions verified. Relaying
the information to my dream study classes, I asked them to
attempt to interpret their sexual dreams based on the new
data I had just presented. The following dreams represent some
of the material I received, including a few of my own. I'll
begin with mine.

FOOLING AROUND

*I'm in bed with an attractive lady and we're both nude.
But all she was doing was playing around with her cats.
Wanting to get down to "business," I told her to quit fooling
around. At that point she gets out of bed with her back
toward me. Bending over, she points to a sore on her rear,
complaining it was painful. Then she gets back into bed
and says to me, "You've been resisting your dreams you
know."*

She was plainly *exposing* the fact that I was finding my
dreamwork to be a *pain in the butt* and was allowing myself

to become distracted with other things. The dream was telling me it was time to quit *fooling around.*

INTERRUPTION

I'm preparing to have sex with a most attractive woman when Dave, my ex-business partner, enters the room on the pretext that he wants to get something out of the next room. I tell him it's OK (even though I know very well he doesn't have anything in there), and ask him to hurry up.

This concerned a business association I was preparing to enter. I was searching my conscience to see if there was a conflict of interest with another client of mine. The delay was causing some concern for the other party. The dream is telling me to *hurry up* and *enter* into it, that *it's OK* and there is *no need to interrupt* this venture any further.

NOT GOING TO MAKE IT

I'm in the back seat of an automobile in a passionate embrace with an old girlfriend. I'm touching her vagina through her underwear, knowing we're not going to have intercourse.

I knew this dream involved my present long-standing relationship. We were both trying to integrate our differences yet we were unable to control the situation, hence the back seat which represented *taking a back seat* in a matter. Being *in the driver's seat* denotes control. Her underwear indicated her deeper feelings, a barrier *I could not penetrate.* We separated in less than a year.

Now, some dreams from our group members with their own interpretations:

I'm with my herbalist, and we're walking down the beach together. We stop and he throws a blanket over us. Still standing, we begin to have sex. He climaxes rather quickly and I ask him, why? He says it's because he's fifty-seven years old (Not his true age). I'm concerned that his wife will find out.

SHIFT

Now we're inside his house and his wife is standing very close to him, looking at me like she knew what happened.

"I feel this dream reflects the *hidden* effects of the herbs I have been taking. The dream shifts from the hidden to the obvious. While they don't make me feel as good as sex does, I do feel much better. For a while I wasn't sure, but now *my suspicions are confirmed.* It's been about two months since I started taking them, possibly *fifty-seven* days, I'm not sure."

This is also another good example of how a shift works. From the hidden, symbolized by the blanket, which can be taken to mean *undercover*, to the wife who *knows* that an integration took place, indicating the obvious.

The next dream is again about health and is also untitled.

I'm making love with a tall, tan blond man at the gym. He seems to be a very hyper type of person. Later, I find out I'm pregnant. He's happy, as he wants to have a child, but I'm worried because I don't know if it's his or my husband's. Now I see a large wooden barrel containing different types of baby bottles. I want to be happy but instead I'm feeling anxious.

"I'm sure this dream has to do with the fact I'm considering joining a gym. The blond man looked very athletic so he probably represented the gym. I'm pregnant by this idea but I don't know how happy my husband will be since I will be gone three nights a week. Part of the program I'm interested in includes aerobics, which may explain the hyperactivity. I can select from several different programs, which I'm sure are represented by the baby bottles. Truthfully, I am feeling anxious, but I didn't think it was affecting my happiness."

OH! OH! TOM

I'm in bed with Tom Selleck. He makes love to me real nice. I thought that being a celebrity might make him less of a lover, but it didn't. I asked him why he was with me, and he replied it was because I was so calm. He said it had been a long time since he had been with a calm woman.

"I think this was my husband in disguise. He told me the other day how calm I've been lately. I attribute it to the fact that I've been meditating more. My involvement with dreamwork has led me to do some private investigation of myself and Tom Selleck plays the role of a private investigator on television. I must admit, I do find him attractive. I guess maybe I'm finding myself more attractive."

DESPERATE

Running through a wheat field, I'm looking for a man to have sex with. I can't find one and the urge is overwhelming. I thought I'd even be willing to pay a twenty-year-old, if I could find one.

"I'm allergic to wheat. In the dream I feel the need to climax or *get off*, which I'm sure means to get off the wheat. I had wheat cereal for breakfast the morning before the dream and I felt lethargic for half the day. Maybe it's something I've had for *twenty years*, but I'm no longer willing to *pay the price*."

The above examples were selected primarily for their brevity. I believe they are well-suited in helping to point out that sexual dreams and the messages they contain may be entirely separate from one another.

It is well-known that in ancient Greece people journeyed to dream temples for the purpose of incubating a healing dream. Because of sexual symbols found in the ruins, researchers understandably felt that these people for the most part were seeking to be healed from some sort of sexual dysfunction. Dr. Garfield again states:

"Researchers suspect that the practice of incubation originally had the cure of sterility as its chief purpose. Many of the priests assumed that some type of sexual union with a god or goddess occurred while the pilgrim slept at the temple: sometimes literal sexual union took place in the form of sacred prostitution. The numerous healing cults of the ancient world are believed to have evolvd from the treatment of sexual inadequacy. (If this is so, the sacred snake of Asclepius may take on additional meaning, as it does in psychoanalysis, as the male sex organ, in this case a part of the god.)"[12]

What if the temple priests knew full well of the integrative healing power of dreams, and that any physical, mental or emotional disorder would show up in a dream as a yin or yang imbalance? If this were so, then it is quite probable that their knowledge also extended into recognizing that sexual dreams do not necessarily have to do with sex, but with an imbalance of polarities. A dream could easily point out where the imbalance lay and possibly how to correct it. Of course, sexual symbolism would make the dream far easier to interpret, so why not attempt to prompt a sexual dream? By exposing the would-be dreamer to sexual and erotic stimuli, such a dream could readily be incubated.

5

$\mathcal{P}$sychic $\mathcal{D}$reams:

PRECOGNITIVE DREAMS

Precognitive dreams reveal future situations, reflecting probable conditions presently shaping or forming. Although it is possible for a negative situation to occur, we should not necessarily accept such dreams at face value. The only ones we hear about are those that come true. My guides say that many precognitive dreams don't come true. This is because our tomorrows are shaped by the choices and decisions we make today, and as a rule, free will allows us to change our future direction at any given moment. I believe such dreams are warnings, allowing us an opportunity to take a different direction and change the course of our lives.

Occasionally, precognitive dreams reveal what appears to be an unalterable destiny, one where we perceive the future, but are unable to intervene. This often occurs in cases concerning others, usually the death of close friends or relatives. I have found it can also extend to our pets as well. Once, I dreamt of two cats, one white, the other black. The black one was sitting on a box-like pedestal when the white cat appeared. They began to fight and after a brief struggle the black cat ran off and the white one took its place on the pedestal. I interpreted the dream as having to do with integration, symbolically depicting aspects of my yin and yang.

Later that day, I arrived home to find my recent ex-girlfriend's black cat stretched out dead in the driveway, where she crawled after being hit by a car. Eventually, my guides revealed the cat's death symbolized the end or "death" of our relationship. I think the dream disguised itself in such a manner as to prevent me from interfering and in some way changing the outcome.

There are two basic types of precognitive dreams. One deals with situations directly affecting the dreamer, encompassing anything of a personal nature, positive or threatening. The other occurs when the dreamer is in touch with the collective, dreaming of future events on a local, national or global level, having little, if any, direct bearing upon the dreamer.

Wanting to learn more about precognitive dreams, I asked my guides to describe their frequency and function.

WHEN A PERSON IS OUT OF TIME AS IN THE DREAM STATE, OR OUT OF THE BODY, POSSIBILITIES RANGING FROM PAST TO PRESENT TO FUTURE CAN BE SEEN RATHER EASILY. IT DOES NOT REQUIRE A GREAT DEAL OF ABILITY TO PULL THROUGH A FUTURE POSSIBILITY AND REFLECT IT IN A DREAM. THIS IS WHY PEOPLE OF ALL LEVELS OF ADVANCEMENT CAN HAVE VERY ACCURATE PRECOGNITIVE DREAMS. WHEN OUTSIDE OF THE TIME FRAME, THEY ARE CAPABLE OF VIEWING TIME AS A SERIES OF POSSIBILITIES IN WHICH THEY NEED NOT MAKE THE DISTINCTION BETWEEN PAST, PRESENT AND FUTURE.

"How is one possibility recognized as being greater than the other?" I asked.

CERTAIN VIBRATORY PATTERNS SET UP IN FAVOR OF A FUTURE POSSIBILITY WILL STAND

OUT STRONGER IN THEIR ENERGY. AS TO HOW OFTEN THEY OCCUR . . . THE FREQUENCY DEPENDS ON VARIOUS FACTORS. A PERSON WILL HAVE A PRECOGNITIVE DREAM WHEN A WARNING IS NECESSARY. THIS IS THE MOST COMMON FORM OF PRECOGNITIVE DREAM. WHEN ONE IS WORKING ON MORE SUBTLE LEVELS SUCH AS STRIVING TO KNOW THE FUTURE OR ATTEMPTING TO MAKE A DECISION, A PRECOGNITIVE DREAM WILL DEVELOP TO AID OR ASSIST THE DREAMER. A PRECOGNITIVE DREAM WILL NOT OCCUR IN A SITUATION WHERE THE KARMA PRECLUDES IT. THAT IS TO SAY, IF A PERSON NEEDS TO WORK THROUGH A PARTICULAR LESSON, WITH NO ASSISTANCE OTHER THAN THE INNER, THEY WILL EITHER NOT RECEIVE A DREAM MESSAGE, OR IT WOULD BE SO VEILED AS TO BE UNDECIPHERABLE. EVEN IF THEY WENT AFTER SUCH ANSWERS ON THE ASTRAL, THEY WOULD BE UNABLE TO BRING THEM BACK TO THE PHYSICAL PLANE.

THE FUNCTION OF THE PRECOGNITIVE DREAM INCLUDES WARNING, THE HERALDING OF AN IMPORTANT EVENT, AIDING IN DECISION MAKING AND ALLEVIATING OF ANXIETIES AT CERTAIN PIVOTAL OR STRESSFUL MOMENTS. A PRECOGNITIVE DREAM IS INTERESTING IN THAT IT REFLECTS PARTICULAR THINGS THE DREAMER WISHES TO KNOW, AS WELL AS SERVING TO WARN OR PROTECT. ALSO, A PRECOGNITIVE DREAM MAY BE DISTINGUISHED FROM A FEARFUL DREAM BY THE FACT THAT A PRECOGNITIVE DREAM USUALLY DOES NOT REPEAT ITSELF AS DOES ONE BASED UPON FEAR.

On the surface, a precognitive dream appears to be like any other dream. Occasionally, a feeling will arise either within the dream or upon recalling it, giving us an inkling of its importance. Unfortunately, in most cases we never know for sure if the dream is precognitive until after the fact. One individual, an avid fisherman, always dreamt of hooking a big fish before landing a contract. After dreaming of a good catch while fishing, he immediately knew the following day would be profitable.

Once, when working in a jewelry store, I dreamt I was a female, and a male was making threatening advances toward me. I felt I was about to be raped, but saw two policemen approaching. The man ran off and I told the police what happened. The next day we had an armed robbery and I was forced at gunpoint to lie on the floor while the thieves relieved me of my wallet. After cleaning out the store, the four men escaped. Later, I gave my statement to the detectives who interviewed us. Upon arriving home that evening, I looked at my dream notes from the night before and found the one I just described.

It is customary for me to hastily scribble out my dreams in the morning. Later, I transcribe and neatly enter them into my dream journal, along with my interpretation. Without a past experience to associate it with, I doubt I would have interpreted this dream as being precognitive. About a year later I had a similar dream. Alerted by my last experience, I sought out my guides. They told me another robbery was contemplated, planned to take place while I was there. I prepared myself as best I could, not telling anyone. I did not want to alarm the store personnel. This worked out well since event never took place. Later, my guides told me that the individuals who plotted the robbery had at the last minute decided against it.

A similar experience happened once before. I dreamt of

speaking to the owners of a house I recently rented. In the dream they said they were going to give me notice, so their daughter and son-in-law could move in. This event also never occurred and my guides said although it was a distinct possibility at the time, they had since changed their minds— *"THE FUTURE IS ALWAYS SHIFTING AND CHANG-ING."* Since future events are only probable, it's important to be discreet when forewarned of an impending situation, otherwise we may create an embarrassing situation, jeopardizing our future credibility.

In her book *The Inner Eye: Your Dreams Can Make You Psychic,* Joan Windsor tells of a dream she had:

> I open the door to the waiting room and go directly to my office. I notice a large gaping hole in the wall between my office and that of my neighbor's. I say, "Bob, we cannot conduct business in private with this hole here."[1]

The author then awoke "with a sense of apprehension and disorientation." Upon entering her office that morning, she discovered a hole cut in the ceiling by burglars who police said were probably after drugs.

At a time when I was experiencing marital difficulties, I had the following dream:

> *I was riding in an automobile with another couple when the man began to tell me about a boating accident where they had lost their child. It was as if I was transported to the scene at a small river. I spot some debris and an old blanket of mine. I lift it up and I see it's the body of our cat, tangled up in some cords that came from the blanket. I wondered whether he drowned or died of strangulation.*

I instinctively knew this dream foretold of the end of our relationship. Death is almost always an ending of something and one's child usually represents a condition created by its parents (a product of both parties in a marriage relationship). Since we didn't have any children, the dream used our cat as a joint symbol. Sixteen days later I had another dream:

Walking home I brush a tree limb extending out over the sidewalk. A nest fell out that contained two blue robin's eggs. It was full of old leaves, like it had been abandoned.

Three months afterword I decided to move out in a trial separation. We never reconciled, and six months later I filed for divorce.

After narrowly avoiding death, Janice Bayliss turned to the study of dreams. It happened after a friend told her she preferred not to be picked up for work at the usual place. Instead, she suggested to Janice they meet elsewhere. No sooner had they departed from this new location when they heard a tremendous explosion. Returning to the original site, they found a small plane had crashed in the exact spot where they had previously been meeting.

"I stopped the car and stared at Mabel. 'How did you know?' I asked. 'Well,' she said, 'I saw it in a dream last night. I didn't want to tell you because I thought you'd think I was silly to take it seriously.' 'Thank God you acted on it!' I answered."[2]

Bayliss went on to author *Dream Dynamics and Decoding,* and *Sleep on It, the Practical Side of Dreaming.*

TELEPATHIC DREAMS

Telepathy is said to be the communication between minds. Some mistakenly believe it is the ability to read minds. Actually, it is the ability to *sense* how another thinks, and translate those thoughts into words. To sense how another *feels,* is called clairsentience. We are all much more telepathic and clairsentient (sensitive) than we realize. Once I was in the company of others, including a Jungian analyst of my acquaintance who recently earned her doctorate. We were discussing dreams when suddenly this woman's judgmental thoughts almost knocked me to the floor. "Who was I," she thought, "to be encroaching on a subject reserved for experts like herself." That, of course, is my translation since I felt her thoughts rather than read them. For the most part, she remained rather reserved during our conversation, but beneath her smiling countenance, a little volcano was erupting.

Another experience occurred when I was dating Beth. Returning from the movies, I made a joke she thought was funny. Upon arriving back at the house she immediately wanted to share the joke with her roommate. Although her roommate sat quietly and said nothing, I could feel a monumental rage building up within her. I wanted to quiet Beth, but it was already too late. The next instant her roommate interpreting my joke as sexist, flew into a rage. My only surprise was that Beth didn't see it coming.

While completing my studies in Southern California, I often frequented a coffee shop where I would go over my notes. This time, a friend and fellow student was helping by verbally quizzing me in preparation for a forthcoming test. Seated at the counter, I began to feel a strange, discordant energy directed toward us. It came from a man seated next to my friend. I watched as he stared sullenly into his coffee cup. Without warning, he angrily snapped, "Do you have to do that?" Startled, we quickly moved from the counter to a table. I sensed this man was very unstable and in certain situations could even be dangerous.

Negative energies are more easily perceived because they are sharp, so to speak. They have a tendency to stab, jar or wound. Love energy, being more gentle, is subtle. Not that it is any less detectable—it is merely less forceful. A case in point was when Beth's sister was visiting us. I began to think of what a kind and loving person she was, and for an instant my heart went out to her. This occurred while she had her back turned to me, helping to clear off the dinner table. Suddenly, she turned around to face me with a pleasantly surprised look and asked "What did you just do to me?" You can rest assured, she was not the only one surprised, not to mention somewhat embarrassed.

During a time when Kathy and I were learning from "Guide," I felt a strange and unpleasant sensation in my solar plexus. I inquired as to what was causing it. Guide mentioned a particular member of our group and asked me to focus on this person and see what I could determine. Immediately, I sensed this person resented the time she felt "forced" to spend on group projects, feeling it was an imposition. Since I was to blame for this, she directed her anger toward me. After the next group meeting I privately questioned her. After admitting her feelings, I told her she mustn't feel obligated, and there would be no hard feelings if she chose to leave the group. She decided to quit, and to this day we still remain friends. Since then, I have learned to recognize this feeling in my solar plexus, and in some cases ascertain the source. More than once I have made telephone calls to surprised individuals asking them to please refrain from directing their energies toward me.

In many cases it is impossible to tell whether some dreams are precognitive, astral or telepathic. On January 7, a student had this dream she felt was precognitive:

A black man who is a teacher does something wrong and angers his supervisor. She wants him imprisoned but someone convinces her just to put him in a detention camp for a while. It's obvious she resents him. Although she is his superior, she doesn't have much education and is always trying to prove herself.

"On February 23, I discovered my supervisor wanted to fire me over some mistakes I made. She made her decision around the time I had my dream. My manager convinced her to put me on probation instead. I feel this dream reveals her motives in wanting to fire me. Her resentment stems from feelings of inferiority. This all took place behind my back, without my being consciously aware of it. My supervisor's feelings were unknown to me at the time. The dream, I feel, gave me some inside information that I would not have otherwise gained."

While this dream appears to be precognitive, it is actually telepathic. My feeling is that the dreamer probably psychically tuned in to what was taking place on or around January 7, and this was replayed in the dream. There is also the possibility an astral encounter took place with her superiors at that time. I also believe my dreams concerning the armed robbery and being evicted, were more likely telepathic, as was perhaps Ms. Windsor's dream.

Telepathy increases with close ties. Friends, family members and spouses share a common love bond. Their concern for each other and frequency of contact tends to strengthen that bond, increasing their sensitivity toward one another. The metaphysical axiom "Thoughts are things" cannot be emphasized strongly enough. There is an area (subplane) of the physical plane known as the *Mental Reflecting Ether,* where these thoughts or thoughtforms gather. When we are in deep meditation or asleep, our mental bodies become more finely attuned with this etheric field. If there are any thoughtforms there—generated by others concerning us—we will immediately become aware of them. If this occurs as we sleep, it usually results in either a precognitive or telepathic dream.

By thinking of ourselves as generating a particular frequency, we may better understand how this mechanism operates. When someone thinks of us strongly enough, or in a manner that will somehow touch our lives, they enter our receptive frequency. Usually, the waking conscious mind is too preoccupied to notice, although many sensitive individuals claim they sometimes *feel* when another is thinking of them.

ASTRAL DREAMS

Parapsychology is now probing a field long known to yogis, mystics and the metaphysical world at large. Astral projection, often referred to as an out-of-body experience, has recently generated enough publicity to capture the attention of the general public. The astral body, composed of an electromagnetic field, surrounds and interpenetrates the physical body. Having the exact appearance as its physical counterpart, it is capable of separation at certain times. When it does detach, it takes with it the consciousness of the individual. This separation occurs when an individual is either asleep, unconscious, in a deeply relaxed state, or dead. Although identical to its mortal equivalent, it carries none of the physical blemishes or disfigurations that one might have.

There are two ways in which we can leave our bodies. One is consciously and the other unconsciously. I have experienced both and might quickly add that conscious astral projection is not for the novice, or one who does not have a good working knowledge of this metaphysical area. The method I use to induce conscious astral projection is to put myself into a trance state. The mind remains awake but empty, while the body sleeps. Consciously leaving your body at the speed of thought can be a frightening enough experience in itself, not to mention the type of place where you may wind up. Because we assume our astral body at death, such an experience may evoke past memories of prior death experiences. On the other hand, unconscious astral projection occurs naturally during sleep, instinctively accepted (within that state) as a normal function, just like dreaming.

Dreams involving seeing or visiting with deceased friends or relatives are commonplace, and are usually genuine astral experiences. Interdimensional meetings between loved ones are more likely to happen than not . . . unless of course, they would induce fear among those of this plane. No one on the other side wishes to frighten those they love. I think many people experience such events and don't recall them. Having had such experiences myself, I remember one occasion when I visited my uncle and legal guardian, who died of a stroke three years prior:

I found myself in a beautiful place. It reminded me of an extravagant mall, unenclosed and decorated with fountains, waterfalls and exotic plants. There were two levels of shops containing everything imaginable. I walked up some stairs to the upper level and into a cafe, taking a seat outside on the veranda. This afforded me a view of the wide, tiled walkway below, where I watched the milling crowd. The colors were vivid and everything was much sharper and brighter than normal. I knew where I was and why I was there. Two women, engaged in conversation nearby, invited me to join them. I felt their friendly warmth, but declined, explaining I was waiting for someone. Looking back down to the passing crowd below, I saw an acquaintance of mine with his wife and child. They died when their private plane crashed about eighteen months previous. I felt my uncle's presence as he approached. The happiness he radiated cannot be described in words. We spoke for a long time and I remember asking why we met here instead of on the plane he was on presently. He said I couldn't handle the vibrations there, and arranged for us to meet at this location.

Some levels of the astral plane are in many respects

counterparts of the physical. Many experiences on the physical plane are a re-enactment of what previously took place on the astral while we slept. This explains, in part, dream synchronicity or meaningful coincidence. It can also help to explain certain deja vu experiences where the dreamer does not consciously remember the astral encounter, but feels a certain familiarity with a particular person, situation or event.

The astral body, sometimes referred to as the desire body, is drawn to areas of the astral plane in keeping one's immediate level of consciousness. It is a place where lovers meet with lovers, students with teachers, businessmen with their associates and friends with friends. If you think intently about someone before you go to sleep, and if they are willing, you will probably meet with them on the astral. This is what we consider an astral event, and usually occurs in the early part of slumber. Quite difficult to recall, it can be dim recollection of a face or of having spoken to someone, or being somewhere, but being unable to remember who or where. Our subconscious however, is fully aware of what took place and will replay the event back to us in a dream, just as if it occurred on the physical plane. This is what we call an astral dream, easily distinguished from an astral event by its rich symbolic content, which the latter lacks.

An illustration to demonstrate this distinction once again involves cats. My wife and I went for a two week vacation leaving our pets behind. Having no one to care for them, we left them inside, with what we thought was ample food, water, and litter. Toward the end of our stay, we began to wonder about them. That evening as I slept, I remember astrally projecting to the house to check on them. Seeing they were not in good shape, I then had the following dream:

DREAM 1.

A catfish was flopping alongside a swimming pool. I recognized it as our gray cat. I picked her up and placed her back in the water, where she swam around in a happy and contented manner.

Immediately upon awakening, I knew our cats were out of water. Remembering the end of the dream, I was not overly alarmed, but felt we should soon start heading back. We arrived home to find both cats suffering from dehydration. An unforeseen extreme hot spell occurred, causing them to drink more water than anticipated. The symbols from the dream, taken at my brother's house where we were staying, came from the previous day's events. He had caught a dozen or so trout, and placed them in his unchlorinated swimming pool, keeping them as "pets."

A dream student whose husband was away on business had this dream:

DREAM 2.

I dreamt I was talking to my husband about the car. He is unhappy, saying that it needs drain cleaner. I awoke concerned about him, sensing he may be upset about the car, that something might be wrong with it.

"That morning, my husband called to tell me he was at a garage and had to kill three hours while having the radiator *drained* and the hoses replaced. It seems one of them sprang a leak, and not wanting to take any chances, he was having them all replaced."

The next dream is slightly more complex. The events leading up to it began after a rather tense discussion with one of my group members after a weekly study session in my home. My counseling was met with rather strong resistance and—without any intent on my part—hurt feelings. Upon falling asleep that evening, I found myself in a heated discussion with this person on the astral. Later, I re-entered my body and awoke with the details of the astral encounter still fresh in my mind. Upset over my advice, this student met with me in an out-of-body state, and proceeded to tell me off, becoming belligerent and argumentative. Unable to penetrate her defensive shield, I returned to my body, awakening to feel her anger still with me. Falling back to sleep, I then proceeded to have the following dream:

DREAM 3.

Angry Iranians were demonstrating. When the demonstration was over the shah told me to remove the solid gold chain that went around the courtyard. It surprised me the crowd didn't recognize the chain as gold and take it. Removing a length of it, I put it in my coat pocket and hung it up in a closet in my bedroom. In doing so, I noticed a man and a woman on the bed having sex. She, fully dressed in Muslim garb, had positioned herself on top, and became increasingly more excited until she finally climaxed. I left and went to the courtyard where they both appeared. The man was angry and threatened me with his sword. The woman called the guards and they chopped him up with their swords.

My analysis was fairly easy since I remembered the astral event. I interpreted the first sentence to mean *I ran* from an *angry demonstration.* I felt she *didn't recognize the value* of what I had to say (the gold chain) and so I *hung it up.* Seeing me do this made her feel like she had *come* out *on top* in our exchange or *intercourse.* The heavy clothing represented *heavy material* desires. The gold chain surrounding the courtyard symbolized the *strength* my advice could give her, which went *unrecognized.* The Shah was the *wiser part* of myself telling me to quit. She saw me as threatening her beliefs and verbally *chopped me up*, as I was the male figure with whom she had intercourse.

We do not always dream of every astral experience, just

as we do not dream about every physical event. I find I only dream of a small percentage of my astral encounters, although it is quite possible I am not recalling many of them.

DREAM 4.

One time I was having an astral conversation with a young woman I knew from work. She was telling me there was something wrong "down there," indicating her female area. I was somehow able to see inside to her uterus, where I found five or six little lumps, each about the size of a pea. I felt they were cysts.

Remembering this when I awoke, I wondered how she would react if I approached her with such a delicate matter. I decided to simply confront her and hope for the best as I have never had a problem with being candid.

The opportunity came the following morning when I found her alone in the coffee room. I simply came right out and asked her if she was experiencing any female problems. If she said no, my intention was to suggest a checkup, saying I had a dream that was probably "nothing," but might be worth considering. At first she thought I was joking and responded with a deft rejoinder. But as I persisted, her demeanor changed. Staring at me with a combined look of fear and amazement, she admitted to seeing a gynecologist the day before. Some tissue samples were taken for a biopsy and she would know the results later in the week. I told her not to worry, that they were not malignant. She asked me how I knew and I simply told her I had a *dream*, all the while wondering if I hadn't frightened the poor thing into thinking I was the devil or something.

She accepted the dream explanation however, and the matter was kept confidential. She did not want anyone at work knowing of her problem. Later, she told me she got "goose bumps all over" after I told her of my "dream." I find people are much more receptive to dreams than to such things as astral projection. Almost two months later, she underwent surgery and had the lumps which tests had shown to be fibroid tumors, removed.

Dream One could easily have been mistaken as being precognitive, and Dream Two telepathic. Dream Three could be misunderstood to relate solely to the previous day's events, leading me to believe my feelings ran deeper than I thought. And Dream Four could also have been misconstrued as telepathic, had I no knowledge of the astral plane. This is why I feel that correct dream analysis must take astral dreams into account. The role they play in our lives is of sufficient importance to warrant their consideration.

6

Dreamwork

The most common complaint I have heard from beginning dreamwork students is the inability to remember their dreams. Those having problems recalling their dreams will find that interest is the greatest stimulus there is. **YOU MUST BE INTERESTED!** It is quite possible you have programmed yourself to dismiss your dreams as being too weird to have any meaning, containing both nonsense and trivia. On the other hand, the dream message may contain something you do not wish to see and are unconsciously blocking it from your mind. Normally, however, all it takes is a little practice. One trick is to take notes immediately upon awakening, but before you are fully awake. Prolong that half-awake state for as long as possible while jotting down your impressions. If there is nothing to recall, write down your feelings, especially those you first had upon awakening. Then close your eyes and try to visualize different scenes, parading them across your mind.

Animals, fish and insects are common symbols, so be sure to include them in your morning review. Think of outdoor scenes such as a tree or a forest, a lake, mountains, fields or clouds. Then switch to indoor scenes, a house, furniture, a particular room or inside a car, bus or other vehicle. Next, try activities like swimming, boating, fishing and so on.

Continue with clothes, tools and anything else you can think of, including people. Begin with those closest to you. While such a review may appear tedious and lengthy, it should take less than five minutes and the results could be quite rewarding.

Sometimes the dream is right on the tip of our minds, so to speak, mocking us with its elusiveness. Then, there are other occasions when we can only recall a fragment and nothing more. When this occurs, it is important to maintain that half-awake state. If we lose it, it is almost impossible to retrieve. One way to determine if you are unconsciously blocking your dreams is by looking at your feelings upon awakening. If you find some that weren't there the night before, the chances are you have set up a block. This can be overcome by convincing yourself that censuring a disturbing or upsetting dream does little to alleviate the problem. One way to do this, is by having a little "heart-to-heart talk" with your subconscious mind, telling it you are ready to accept your dream mind's offerings and appreciate whatever advice it can give. Try not to distance yourself from the feelings the dream evokes. Stirring up the emotions is often necessary to unload what we have stored up. To deprive ourselves of this experience causes us to lose a wonderful opportunity for integrative balancing.

There have been periods where I have recalled my evening repertoire with ease. Other times, I have the greatest difficulty recalling even a fragment. Since "dream experts" are not supposed to have this sort of problem, I approached my guides with it.

YOU WILL FIND THAT THE DREAMS YOU RECALL MOST CLEARLY ARE DREAMS THAT HAVE THE MOST EFFECT UPON YOUR WAKING STATE.

SOMETIMES A PORTION OR FRAGMENT WILL STAND OUT MORE VIVIDLY THAN THE REST. IN

SOME INSTANCES THAT WILL BE ALL YOU WILL
BE ABLE TO RECALL. IT IS BECAUSE THAT
PORTION REVEALS SOMETHING THAT YOU CAN
CLEARLY RELATE TO IN YOUR WAKING
CONSCIOUSNESS.

YOU WILL ALSO FIND A CORRESPONDENCE
BETWEEN BIORHYTHMS AND DREAM RECALL.
WHEN YOUR BIORHYTHMS ARE LOW YOU WILL
EXPERIENCE GREATER DIFFICULTY IN RECAL-
LING YOUR DREAMS. WHENEVER THE PHYSI-
CAL BODY IS TIRED OR STRESSED TO THE POINT
WHERE YOU SLEEP MORE SOUNDLY, DREAM
RECALL IS LESSENED.

THERE ARE PLANETARY ASPECTS AND CON-
DITIONS AS WELL, WHICH AFFECT DREAM
RECALL, BUT THESE ARE MINOR IN COMPAR-
ISON TO THAT WHICH WE HAVE JUST
DISCUSSED.

While there seems to be enough evidence to support the
fact that we do not remember our dreams well enough when
we are overly tired, I never connected it with our biorhythms.
A final point to remember is that alcohol and drugs, whether
medicinal or otherwise, tend to inhibit dream recall.

PROGRAMMING

The following suggestions for recalling and recording your
dreams are certainly open to revision and elaboration. There
are no hard-and-fast rules, so don't be afraid to experiment
and find what works best for you.

You must convince yourself that you truly want to remember
your dreams. The best time to do this is just before falling
asleep. Keeping in mind the benefits involved, repeat a one-
line suggestion to yourself such as: *I will remember my dreams*

upon awakening. Soon, the subconscious mind will get the message and your dream recall will improve. The best way to induce dreams is by relaxing. Go to bed relaxed, not tired. Contemplation on a given subject always induces dreams. Fasting and meditation usually produce vivid dreams. You may also program yourself to dream about anything you wish to have answered. This is called *incubation,* and is covered in the following section.

If you choose to program yourself to awaken immediately after a dream, you will be rewarded by a very fresh and vivid impression. If you have trouble going back to sleep, reword your programming to include that you will quickly and easily fall back to sleep. Alarms are to be avoided, as they tend to blast the dream away. Some people use mellow music stations on their clock radios, but I find the music becomes distracting rather quickly, as does shutting off any device.

INCUBATION

Dream incubation is an ancient art. This method is particularly well-covered in Gayle Delaney's *Living Your Dreams.*[1] In order to incubate a dream properly, the issue must first be important enough to attract the attention of the subconscious or superconscious mind. Second, you must be willing to work on it, keeping it down to a single issue. Choose an evening when you are not overly tired or distracted. There are a series of steps to take in order to obtain proper results. The dream mind must in some way be prompted and the following has been used successfully by many dream students, including myself:

1. Pose your question concisely, choosing a meaningful issue.
2. Sleep in a "sacred" place. This means that if possible, sleep in a place other than where you are accustomed. My sacred place is on the sofa. Perhaps when we sleep in a different place we do not sleep as deeply, thus remembering our

dreams more clearly. Purists may choose to burn incense, play spiritual or "new age" music and possibly chant.

3. Pray or meditate, calling upon your spiritual guides, your higher self, the masters or the religious deity of your choice.

4. Now concentrate on the issue. Try to examine each alternative and every possible outcome. Allow your feelings to enter in the process.

5. Lie back, repeating your question as you fall asleep.

I have modified the final step in that I use autosuggestion coupled with visualization. First, I repeat my question or phrase suggesting I will receive a constructive answer. Then I move into the visualization part. Let's say, for instance, you want to know if you are going to be selected to fill a newly vacated position at your office. Perhaps you are unsure you'll like it, or if you will be capable. Just before falling asleep, visualize yourself filling this new position and carrying on with your assigned duties and responsibilities. If entering into a partnership or relationship, visualize yourself in that environment. After a moment, blank out the scene and hold in your mind the character of a question mark, while wondering whether you will enjoy this position. Here you are speaking to the subconscious in its own language, providing many interesting and creative experiments, which should offer equally interesting results.

In hypnotic progression, I have led clients into the future, having them live out a role they are contemplating accepting, to see how well they like it. Having helped many to make decisions regarding their future in this respect, I believe the same results can be had with dreams. Dreamworkers, for the most part, find incubated dreams more vivid and easier to recall than spontaneous ones.

The following dream, provided by a dream student, is the result of incubation. An electrologist, she was thinking of branching out or extending her services to include *camouflage makeup,* which cosmetically hides exposed scar tissue. Most often applied after cosmetic or plastic surgery, it is a relatively new field. She slept in her own bed and used only autosuggestion and visualization. This dream occured after four successive nights of using this method:

> *I'm talking to a woman who is standing in a room full of other women. She asks me what I do for a living and I tell her that I'm an electrologist, but I'm also thinking of doing paramedical makeup. She says that is a good idea because of the large amount of people having plastic surgery these days.*

As in this example, most incubated dreams appear to be very direct and clear in their response. They enable the dreamer to gain information that would otherwise be inaccessible, and provide valuable assistance in any area of one's life.

RECORDING

Dreams are best recorded by writing them down as opposed to using a tape recorder. Keep pencil and paper close at hand. A penlight is less disturbing than a lamp if you are awakening at night. Night-writer pens and clip-on book lamps work very well. I found it cumbersome to try to hold a penlight in one hand and write with the other while in bed, so my wife found me a plastic clipboard with a little battery-operated swivel lamp attached. It serves my needs quite adequately. I use a legal pad to scribble out my notes and later in the day or evening, neatly transfer them into my dream journal. Some people create a book out of each dream, superfluously writing out each little detail, thus making recording a miserable chore. While it is important to record a dream accurately, it need not be excessively wordy. Condense your dream into a precise and concise story, going over it your mind line by line as you write it down. This is done while you are transferring it into your dream journal. Be sure to date and title your dream; it makes for easy future reference.

I find it best to wait awhile before attempting to interpret a dream. When we attempt to decipher a dream while still too close to it, we find ourselves lost in the story and unable to read the message. Detachment and objectivity help to make the symbols more revealing, enabling us to spot hidden messages rather quickly. After having unraveled as much as possible in this manner, we may then try associating more with the feeling level or theme of the dream. This gives us the opportunity to explore both sides with greater ease and accuracy, without having one distract us from the other. As we uncover various symbols we may then include them in a dream dictionary. A dictionary is not only helpful for reference, it allows us to gain insight into the language of our dreams. My dictionary consists of a hardbound diary that I have alphabetized with index tabs. You can easily find something suitable at your local stationery store. Even an alphabetically indexed address book will do.

DREAM TERMINOLOGY

One of the first things to watch for in a dream is *displacement.* This is when the dream figure is out of place or disguised, appearing as someone or something totally different. Freud felt that displacement occurs when we are resistant to the dream message. Consequently, we disguise the figure in an attempt to hide it. Many psychologists today disagree, feeling displacement in a dream does not necessarily signify resistance. It may be we associate a particular quality with someone other than who we are dreaming about—this is found in a good percentage of our dreams. One woman dreamt she was with Robert Redford, only to remember upon awakening that many people commented on how much her husband looks like Robert Redford. Also, as pointed out earlier in the section on aspects, we often project our own traits or characteristics, displacing them onto someone or something else.

Word play is another important aspect to watch for. A play on words is common in most dreams. I once dreamt of going to the Philippines before taking a short vacation in the mountains where I got my *fill of pines.* Using *syllabification,* or dividing the word into syllables, I uncovered its meaning. Another dreamer who was married and having an affair, dreamt she and her lover were eating cantaloupe in one segment of her dream, telling her she *can't elope* with this man.

Proper nouns usually indicate a strong message. I sometimes dream of an old grammar-school classmate named William Wilson, who represents my *will* or *will power.* Market Street may represent something you're *in the market for,* while Grand Avenue may signify an excellent approach in a particular *avenue of your life.* Look for word play with other nouns as well. A taxi could suggest something that's taxing you, a suitcase can represent a case involving a lawsuit, and a freeway can mean an unimpeded direction. Slang expressions, metaphors and cliches are also often used in dreams. I have come across many, such as: *asleep at the switch, stabbed in the back, screwed, shafted, railroaded, strings attached, chicken, in the dark, a piece of cake,* and *timid as a mouse.* Don't forget homonyms like mail meaning male, sun meaning son or to meaning two. Homographs are two words spelled the same but have different meanings like stump, mine, lean and barge. Occasionally we will get a *composite* to give us a clue in a displacement dream. For a brief second someone else's face superimposes over the face of the displaced dream character, revealing its identity, or at least a connection. Sometimes the composite does not readily reveal itself. I once dreamt of a creature that appeared as a cross between a deer and an ox. It was precognitive of meeting a person who is now a very good friend. A shy and gentle dear, but very strong in her character and convictions.

ASSOCIATION METHOD

Freud first employed what we call the *"free association method"* to uncover hidden motivating or influencing factors at work on an unconscious level. In dreams, we use it to determine the meaning of symbols. Every dream contains certain key symbols, clues that catch the interpreter's eye by standing out more distinctly than the rest. They are found in both the character and what the character is doing. In the association method, we isolate the characters and the actions by writing them down separately. Then, we attempt to associate them with something else, including any feelings we may have. Such feelings can relate to feelings we had within the dream or feelings evoked while interpreting it. If we cannot connect any feelings to the symbol we either leave it alone or write *none* after it. If we choose to come back and work on it at a later time, we may wish to put a question mark in that spot. Since positive and negative are but two sides of the same coin, we can—by determining which side is up—isolate constructive and destructive feelings. Additionally, it enables us to pinpoint areas in our lives that may be giving us trouble, as well lending corrective or positive advice. Here is a dream I had a few years ago:

LEMON TREE

My wife was picking a lemon off our lemon tree. It wasn't ripe and I told her not to pick it. She picked the fruit and squeezed it in disbelief. Although it was still somewhat green, it was very soft and mushy.

Breaking the dream down into three catagories may help to decipher its meaning. If we can make an association, or uncover any feelings revolving around the dream symbol, we list them alongside (as described above) under the appropriate heading.

CHARACTERS & OBJECTS	ASSOCIATIONS	FEELINGS
my wife	my yin side	none
lemon	sour	no good

ACTIONS		
picking a lemon	a bad selection	something wrong
squeezing it	testing it	not ripe

THEME: making a selection.
PLOT: picking fruit.
POLARITY FOCUS: yin.

The fact the lemon was soft and mushy suggests it is bad. My yin side can represent my intuition. The day prior to the dream I had been looking at used cars. I test-drove a fairly new model with exceptionally high mileage and was considering purchasing it. After analyzing the dream, however, I chose not to buy it.

Actually, the association method consists of simply associating one thing with another, but unlike Freud's free association, where you use whatever first comes into your mind, we employ a slightly different method. The plot of a dream always revolves around the characters and what they are doing. This is where we must focus our attention. When we consider all we have learned thus far concerning dream symbology, the association we make is not so free or random. I knew my wife was not picking lemons to bake lemon meringue pie. As she is representative of my female side, she could well symbolize my intuitional nature. I also knew dreams love to incorporate metaphors, slang expressions and cliches. This narrows down the field of association immensely.

The associations we make are not limited just to one idea. We may use our first association as a steppingstone, reaching out infinitely further, in a series of associations known as a *chain.* Let's say you dream of your Uncle Bob. You have the figure, Bob, and your first association is that he is your uncle. Now we associate uncle. An uncle is a relative, symbolic of someone or something in close *relationship* to the dreamer. Your uncle Bob drives a red sports car and so do you, which gives us another relationship. You know he is not a good driver and you are scared to ride with him. Lately, your spouse (yet another relationship) has commented on your driving habits. In other words, it's all <u>related</u> to your *driving like Uncle Bob.*

Let's try some other examples using the association method, first picking out the keys, then using our current knowledge of dreams to associate the keys with different meanings.

FRENCH BREAD

I *'m in a* **park** *by* **Disneyland** *at a table where the* **food** *is* **priced** *very* **low.** **I** *grab a* **plate** *and start to* **help myself.** **I** *put two pieces of* **French bread on** *the* **plate** *and* **one falls to** *the* **ground.**
SHIFT
I **now** *have a young* **black boy** *with me and we are sitting with a lot of other people outside. The boy decides to* **urinate** *right then and there,* **leaving a big puddle. I was very upset.**

CHARACTERS & OBJECTS	ASSOCIATIONS	FEELINGS
park	picnic	fun
	food	
	recreation	
Disneyland	entertainment	fun
	social activity	
	food	
food	nourishment	good
plate	dish of food	?
	to dish out	?
French bread	dining out	pleasurable
ground	bottom level	?
	foundation	?

	dirt	negative
boy (yang)	developing aspect	?
	immaturity	negative
black	hidden	?
	dark	?
	subconscious	?
puddle	a mess	anger

ACTIONS

Helping myself to low priced food.	fast food	negative
Half falls to the ground.	half-dirty	negative
Urinating in public.	eliminating in public	embarrassing
I'm upset.	feeling upset	negative

THEME: outdoor recreation.
PLOT: dining.
POLARITY FOCUS: yang.

This is the work of a beginning dream student who already has a working knowledge of symbols, which she put to use in uncovering the meaning of the *black boy, urinating,* and *plate.* The rest of the dream however, was figured out simply by symbol association. As you can see, the dream was dietary. It shifted from the cause to the effect. At first, she interpreted the dream to relate strictly to eating at fast food restaurants, which she did on occasion. But knowing she had a wheat allergy, I carried out the dream a step further. If we take *park* as a space where we park minds, we see that it is near Disneyland, which could represent *dizzyland.* Low-priced food could mean *low-energy* food. French bread would be something to which she is allergic. Half of it falling to the ground could be her reaction of becoming *ungrounded.* In addition, bottom level could represent *bottom line*, which would definitely mean the *foundation* of the dream. It then shifts, and she becomes the little black boy (I now . . . black boy). He is unaware that there's anything wrong with what he is doing, while in actuality he is *creating a big mess*. He represents her decision-making faculty. The theme was outdoors, meaning food she was eating *outside* the home. The *people* represented the public and the last line is a *summation* of how she feels about herself.

While her interpretation was entirely correct, there was still more to be found. The dream not only covered fast foods, but dining out in general. This dream has many good examples of *condensation,* where many meanings are condensed into one symbol. Park, for example, was equated to *picnic,* which through chain association equates to *eating out*. An experience where she chooses to occasionally *park* herself and have *fun*. The boy was *black,* representing her unconscious. In this case she deliberately chose to ignore (make herself unconscious of) the effects of her indulgence, which may be construed as *childish. Dizzyland,* symbolized a physical condition or reaction. A dish or plate usually means something being *dished out*, which she already knew. After going over the dream again she remembered that someone on the other side of the table handed her a plate from a stack. Now it made even more sense. She is being *handed* some advice or it is being *dished out* to her. I cannot emphasize the importance of **not including your assumptions** when you write out your dream. It's easy to think "what's the difference" if you are handed a plate or if you take one? True, this is a small case in point and did not make much difference in the overall interpretation. However, I have spent many needless hours with dreams where portions have been left out, substitutions and assumptions made, or where they have been poorly worded. It can be very misleading, causing either frustration, an incorrect interpretation, or both.

A simpler means of using this method is to underline the keys and number them sequentially. Copy the numbers onto your dream worksheet, each number placed on a different line. Begin with number one, using as many associations as you wish but ultimately reducing them down to one. Don't use any headings, but continue to keep your actions separate from the characters. Rewrite your dream, substituting your associations in place of the original symbols. I will use a recent dream of mine as an example:

BOXED IN

I'm driving[1] *my pickup* **truck**[2] *in the* **right**[3] *hand lane when two* **semis**[4] *in front of me* **collide**[5] **blocking**[6] *off the highway. Behind me a* **train**[7] *runs* **off the track,**[8] *cutting off my rear. I put the truck into* **four-wheel drive**[9] *and leave the road, driving up onto* **higher ground**[10] *where I* **survey the situation**[11] **looking for alternate routes**[12] *A man appears out of nowhere and tells me to* **remember to trust**[13] *I recognize him as a* **spiritual being**[14] *even though he is* **smoking a cigarette**[15] *I thank him for the advice and he disappears.*

Here I have emphasized 15 keys, much more than I would normally use to analyze a dream of this size. The main key of a dream is a centrally linked symbol that when deciphered allows us to rapidly break down the rest. For me, *train* stood out from the others. I usually associate trains with a *train of thought.* Then I see *I'm off the track,* which fits with train of thought. I now have a handle on the dream and will focus my associations in a particular direction. Let's see if I am right.

1. **I'm driving:** in control, a direction I'm taking. (yang)
2. **Truck:** a work vehicle; my working self. (yang)
3. **Right:** correct. (yang)
4. **Semi:** partial; incomplete. (yang)
5. **Collide:** not flowing.
6. **Block:** halt; stop; impede.
7. **Train:** train of thought. (yang)
8. **Off the track:** not on course. (yang)
9. **Four wheel drive:** a different gear; better traction. (yang)

10. **Higher ground:** a higher level.
11. **Surveying the situation:** literal.
12. **Looking for alternate routes:** seeking a different direction.
13. **Remember to trust:** a message.
14. **Spiritual being:** higher self or guide.
15. **Smoking a cigarette:** taking a break. (yang)

THEME: direction.
PLOT: getting stuck.
POLARITY FOCUS: yang.

There is no need for the dreamer to rewrite each key alongside their associations as I have done in this example. I did it so the reader would not have to constantly refer back to the dream. The first sentence of the dream tells me I am blocked in a direction I am taking. There are six symbols in that first sentence. Taking them one by one, I see something I am working on (2), while correct (3), is incomplete (4). A flow is halted (5 & 6). The next sentence tells me my train of thought is "off the track" (7 & 8). I go up to a higher level to "survey the situation," seeking a different direction (9–12). I am given a message to relax, take a break or both (13–15). I do not allow smoking in an area where I am teaching. At *break time,* all the smokers rush for the door. For this reason, I associate smoking with taking a break.

This dream is fairly common in that it does not tell you what it is about. In many instances the dream mind feels the subject is so obvious it need not be included. I do not always agree with that, but in this case it was true. I knew it had to do with writing this book. Now, let's rewrite the dream.

I'm working on my book, headed in the right direction when suddenly my thoughts collide. I'm blocked with nowhere to turn, feeling I'm off the track with my present train of thought. I survey my dilemma from a higher level of consciousness seeking some direction. I'm given the message to trust. Take a break and relax, everything will turn out just fine.

And it did! The strong yang symbolism indicated the problem was with the logical mind rather than the creative. This is because at this point I was deciding what goes in which chapter.

SECTIONING METHOD

This method works especially well when applied to longer dreams. It helps to get to the core of the dream quickly. The dream is sectioned off or divided into smaller messages that can later be expanded into a more complete interpretation.

HAIRCUT

It was the last hour of work, near quitting time. My long blond hair was black in the dream. It was hanging in my face and interfering with my work.

SHIFT

Now I'm at home, cutting my hair short. The next day everyone at work (all females) is surprised and pleased by my short hair. A nurse comes over to me and wants to take a sample of it to make a culture. I was excited and could hardly wait to see if the experimental culture would grow and produce the healing medicine they wanted.

They say that actions speak louder than words; this is particularly true with dreams. The first thing one should look for while scanning are the verbs. *Interfering with my work* is an action that clearly stood out, suggesting this woman was having a problem with her job. I jotted down *problems w/job* in the left-hand margin alongside the first three lines. Cutting hair *is making a change*, it was positive because people were pleased. I then wrote *positive changes* in the margin alongside the first two lines after the shift. A culture is *growth;* the sentence also contains a message that it is associated with *healing.* I now have an overview of the dream telling me that a problem she is having with her job can be changed by changing herself, providing a healthier environment. Now, let's see how she used the association method:

CHARACTERS & OBJECTS	ASSOCIATIONS	FEELINGS
black hair (yin)	negative thoughts	disappointment
co-workers (yin)	self or co-workers	friendship
nurse (yin)	healing or health	none
medicine (yin)	cure or heal	positive
ACTIONS		
near quitting time	nearing time to quit	sadness
black hair in face	hanging onto negative thoughts	anger
interfering with work	literal	anger
cutting hair (yang)	getting rid of interference	relief
taking a sample	sampling	?
making a culture (yang)	growth	positive

This student was of an intermediate level who recognized the dream message long before she finished breaking it down. She was upset and discontented with her job, and on the verge of quitting. Equating hair with thoughts (since they both grow from of one's head), she saw herself as being in a negative situation. The dream is telling her all she has to do is change her attitude. In this respect, she would cultivate a healthier approach, producing a healing effect upon herself and others. Notice the shift here, from the problem to the solution or from the negative (yin) to the positive (yang).

In the section under Health Dreams in Chapter Four, I mentioned some problems I was having with my teeth. After redoubling my efforts toward oral maintenance, I had the following dream:

> *My wife put some white powder on the Italian tile I recently laid in the dining room. People walking on it created an abrasive action, wearing the patterns down in some spots. Seeing all my work go to waste upset me—I point this out to her.*

My immediate question is, why am I raising hell with my female side? Tile, is of course the key. What comes to mind is ceramic, porcelain, glaze. My teeth? Of course! I occasionally used a mixture of baking soda and salt (abrasive) with my electric toothbrush set on high, which is wearing down the enamel. Why my wife? It does not matter who we are caring for—ourselves or others; nurturance always belongs to the female or yin side.

Most dreams will reflect current situations, although perhaps not always in such an obvious manner as this example. If the dreamer will bear this in mind, it will help to narrow the focus of the dreamwork, and more accurately pinpoint the area of one's life around which the dream revolves. Also, if we have an exceptionally long dream or one that is giving us a problem, we may wish to use what Freud calls *fractional dream interpretation*, where the dreamer quits working on the dream if they feel they are blocked or tired, and cannot make any more headway. Freud felt that whenever we come to an impasse in our analytic work, we are resisting. In such cases the dreamer should pause for a while before continuing, or else put it down entirely and resume at a later date.

ADVANCED DREAMWORK
DIALOGUING

We often put up a barrier between ourselves and our feelings. It serves as a protective shield to insulate us from our emotional sensitivity. Dialoguing is a gestalt technique designed to penetrate this inner defense mechanism by assigning a separate identity to our feelings. In dreamwork, the dream characters are given a voice and allowed to converse with the dreamer. It is a means of focusing on inner conflicts and working through them in a highly creative manner, thus giving dreamwork an added dimension. This advanced technique is very interesting to work with and of great benefit to those who use it.

Traditionally, two chairs are placed facing one another. The subject, playing the role of interrogator, sits in one chair and questions the imagined character sitting opposite, attempting to define who or what it represents. By switching to the opposite chair after the question has been asked, the subject assumes the role of the dream character and answers accordingly.

While I have never used chairs, I do recognize the value in remaining separate from the dream characters. They will not speak freely if we are too emotionally involved with them. In contradistinction, we find most beginners reluctant to identify with these characters as aspects of themselves, thus causing them to encounter difficulty in their dialoguing attempts. We must accept that we are speaking to a separate aspect of ourselves, while remaining emotionally detached.

The following examples have been selected from an advanced dreamwork student.

RIVER OF SADNESS

A story had been written by a man, and I was watching it being played out in detail as if I were watching a movie. It was about two young men who were going to swim upriver to get somewhere, and also to prove that they could do it. On their journey the thin man got caught up in some quicksand and drowned. The other, a heavier-set man, grievingly retrieved the body and somehow took care of it. He then went on swimming. It was night. As he slowly

swam on, he came to a whirlpool and was sucked down.
He also died.

Dreamer: River, who are you?

River: I am the river of your sadness, your fear, your loneliness in the night of your despair. I am made of your tears and your sorrow, and I am treacherous in that I am your undoing.

Dreamer: Young men, why are you swimming in that river?

Young men: We have no choice, you wrote us to do so.

Dreamer: Did I write what your motive was?

Young men: No, we are just two aspects of yourself caught up in your sorrow.

Dreamer: What two aspects?

Thin man: I am your youth, your talent, your interest in love and life. I'm just starting out, immature and unsure of myself. This dies in smothering anger and self-criticism. Once I get caught it just sucks me in. The more I struggle the faster it takes me down.

Dreamer: Who is the other, fatter man?

Fat man: I'm your sensitivity, compassion . . . feeling that the inside of you is beautiful. I'm more mature and developed in you, but I'm swallowed by the whirlpool created by your conflicting feelings. I'm spent and exhausted . . . drained by dealing with your sadness and highly active emotional nature.

As one can see, dialoguing can be highly productive (and in this case very poetic), while giving the dreamer much food for thought. This woman has a strong emotional (yin) imbalance. The males exhibit positive yin qualities, appearing as males because they are emerging expressions, thrusting outward and attempting to establish a foothold. Their struggle for survival is clearly yang, which becomes swallowed up and destroyed by the negative yin.

I am amused at how often I creep into other people's dreams. The next dream proves that my students cannot get rid of me even after they have gone to bed.

OLD EGGS

George was fixing eggs at the stove. He had three pans with three or four eggs in each. I said that was too many to eat. He said he was trying to get rid of the old eggs before they went bad. One large metal pan contained mostly raw egg whites in it. We were going to give them to the cats but then realized it was the yolks they were supposed to have; the whites weren't that good for them. George tried to put a few yolks from another pan in there, but I was worrying that it still wasn't enough to offset the whites.

Dreamer: George, what are you doing?

George: You have to eat all these seed ideas that are going bad in you. I need to cook them up and I'll eat them all if necessary, in order to get rid of them.

Dreamer: Yes, but who are you that you could do that and not be sick? Why can't you throw them out?

George: No, they mustn't be discarded. They must be recognized, worked through by cooking them. If you won't do it, then I will.

Dreamer: Who are you?

George: I'm the higher part of your personality that you're developing by working on yourself.

Dreamer: Why are we feeding egg whites to the cats?

George: The cats are your unconscious. If you relegate your responsibility unconsciously you will suffer for it.

Dreamer: OK, how can I take care of these eggs myself?

George: Work toward integration so you won't have to keep slogging through old uncooked seeds. Don't run from the pain and conflict . . . face it! Draw upon your supreme inner strength and persevere in working toward self-realization.

The advice given in dialoguing is usually direct and to the point. This is a highly advanced technique that requires practice and persistence. You may wish to employ the aid of a second party who plays your role as the dreamer, asking you preselected questions that you prepared in advance. Using this method, you play the role of each of the characters in your dream. Some people feel they can get into it more by closing their eyes. The more common method is simply to write down the question, address it to the dream character and take down the reply.

SIXTH SENSE

Developing a *sixth sense* for interpreting your dreams—while not exactly easy—is far from impossible. I once asked my dream teachers how it was they could so accurately interpret anyone's dreams. I was told that we *know* one another to the same extent we know ourselves. Since these beings know themselves perfectly, they can tune in to each and every one of us, and know us perfectly also. Applying this to myself, I found it to be true. The masters don't dream while in incarnation. This is because they have no unconscious, hidden or repressed side to themselves. They are acutely aware of everything they say or do, and their motive is always selfless. When in incarnation, they are in total command of the subconscious regulatory function of their bodies. Having the ability to lower or raise their blood pressure, heartbeat and body temperature at will, they can exert complete control over their respiratory and nervous systems. This is what we are all evolving toward, and we begin by paying constant attention to ourselves—a silent witness to our behavior, feelings, desires, and particularly our motives.

By perceiving ourselves in this manner, we relate to our dreams more easily. Even the dreams of others become less mysterious. We all essentially know what is good for us and what is not. Every time we deviate from our *good* path we may wish to make a note and see if we dream about it. The following two dreams are part of a dream *series* I recently had.

BAD WIZARD

A strange-looking man dressed in a colorful robe appeared at my door. He told me someone was after him and asked if I would help. I said yes, and let him in. Once inside he magically created a bar and an attractive woman. They were both seated on the bar stools and began to party and carry on. On the bar was a rotisserie with several chickens on it. They were taking the cooked flesh off one and eating it with their fingers. He offered me some and I said "That's a great illusion" as I tasted it. He then offered me a slice of roast beef of which I took a single bite to sample. I somehow realized I let in the wrong person and that the one who truly needed my help was still outside. The impersonator read my mind and tried to prevent me from opening the door. As we struggled I magically created a sword and ran him through the heart whereupon he screamed, then disappeared. I knew he would soon be back. I had to hurry and get my cat. I got in my car and drove to a certain area where I felt she would be. I found her, picked her up in my arms and started to run back to the car. Just then I heard him approaching in the distance. I began to run even faster but felt he was gaining on me.

The chicken and beef were the keys that stood out for me in this dream. Primarily a vegetarian, I occasionally supplement

my meals with a little poultry and fish. During the period
I had this dream, I was in the midst of remodeling my house.
I was so intent upon this project that I did not wish to be
distracted by cooking. I began to send out for Chinese food.
Many of the dishes contained chicken and a few had some
beef. Knowing that I was being "bad" in my dietary choice,
I half expected to have some dreams about it. The magical
theme stemmed from my wife's remark that I was *magically*
transforming the house. While under the *pretext* that I was
too involved with this project, I let in the wrong person
. . . my meat-eating self, which I found appealing. This is
the reason for the *attractive woman*. I had a little *heartburn*
from this food, but paid it no attention. Evidently, *this food
was out to get me* and it was important to get this message
across from my unconscious (the cat), to my conscious self
before it *caught up with me.*

Because I was so involved in my project, I didn't analyze
the dream until several days later, after I had this second dream:

LOST WALLET

*I'm about to be seated at a restaurant when I notice
my wallet is gone. I return to a sleazy hotel where I've
been staying and report my loss to an older woman, who
is the manager. She is behind a closed door with a little
screen in front. I sense she is in a hurry, about to leave.
Another man, somewhat younger than myself, tries to get
in front of me, but I push him aside. I explain my situation
telling the lady I had fifty dollars in the wallet besides
all my identification. She's unsympathetic and belittles my
loss. Then she departs, leaving on a charter bus with a
lot of other elderly women.*

The first line tells me I'm suffering a *loss*, which may have
to do with *food*. I've returned to a *sleazy transient space* where
I'm staying and report my loss. The *older woman* represents
my *old eating habits,* which took me through the first thirty

years of my life. She is doing *little* to *screen* out my food selection. *Fifty* is a five which represents *change and movement,* among other things. I've *changed* or *moved away* from my regular eating habits which became a part of my *identity.* The younger man represents my *newer* healthy *eating habits* that I've *pushed aside.* The last sentence depicts the *course I have chartered: departure.* This is again reiterating the message that I had departed from my usual healthy eating pattern.

Were I less aware of what I was doing, my dreams would have been more difficult to interpret. As it was, they took little effort. I intuitively focused upon particular keys that helped to unravel these dreams rather quickly. I believe it was this awareness that kept these dreams closer to the surface, enabling me to access the message rather effortlessly. By paying equal attention to our outer and inner life, we will enrich both.

When we have two or more dreams revolving around the same issue such as this, they are known as *series* dreams. Once you have a dream journal going, you may wish to look back and see if you can discover any dreams that are in some way connected.

HOLISTIC APPROACH

There is a segment in the dream field that feels that breaking a dream down into "bits and pieces" fragments them to a point where a major portion of the dream is missed or the fullness and richness of the dream is lost. There is another segment that I feel wants to preserve some of the mystery surrounding dreams, giving them something to ponder over which serves to enrich their imaginations. My belief is that one can get too caught up in the flow of the dream and fail to see the mechanics. I have a questioning mind that always wants to know how something works. Movement (motion), whether of the mind or other realms, must have a mechanical principle, functioning either under the law of physics or metaphysics. This applies whether we work as a scientist or alchemist, pragmatist or *dreamer.*

I have attempted to point out that dreams do have a structure, and breaking a dream down into bits and pieces does not necessarily cause us to lose any of its richness or fullness. We all appreciate a well-proportioned human body, but when we can see through to the skeleton, organs and layers of muscle and tissue that make up this body, we discover how it works, appreciating it all the more.

The holistic approach evaluates the dream as a whole, encompassing the intellectual, experiential, and feeling levels. A dream is viewed as an experience and what is sought here is the sum of that experience. Careful attention is paid to the fluidity or movement within the dream. Colors and other symbols are examined, both within the context of the dream and as separate entities. A truly holistic approach will always seek to go beyond the symptom (which in this case is the dream) and find the cause. The methodology cannot be one-sided, focusing primarily upon the fragments or parts, or becoming lost in the flow or movement created when those parts are connected. It is the combination of the two that in my opinion constitutes a genuine holistic approach.

7

The Other Side of Dreaming

SPIRITUAL DREAMS

I dreamt I was in a car driven by a man of somber appearance, dressed in a dark suit. Suddenly, a speeding car appeared to cross our path. I abruptly reached for the wheel, but the car vanished as quickly as it appeared. The man seemed unperturbed. It was then I noticed the small steering wheel, about eight inches in diameter. We arrived at a building and the man mentioned something about being involved with the governor's committee. I followed him into the building where he stopped before an open room, allowing me to enter first. We seated ourselves and he handed me a book, which I opened. It contained a poem:

> *I shot an arrow to the sky*
> *And stood awaiting a reply.*
> *I shot again and heard a cry:*
> *"You shall not know until you die."*

At this time, I was praying to regain control of my life. It was as if some invisible force was governing the direction it was taking, and I wanted to know why. Somehow, this dream set my mind at rest, and now the answer does not seem as important anymore.

We often tend to equate spirituality with religion. Strictly defined, however, it means *of the spirit or soul.* By applying this within the context of a religious framework, we may lose sight of its true meaning—oneness, with the earth and the kingdoms of nature. Oneness entails brotherhood, and our ability to work together in a common cause, regardless of our race or belief. When we work in a loving environment, we all prosper by enriching our souls. Those engaged in the pursuit of such an environment are, in my opinion, spiritual beings. Be they agnostic or atheist, they follow the dictates of their soul.

Being spiritual simply implies goodness, extending toward humanitarianism—motivated to help, uplift and inspire others, solely because it's the right thing to do, without thought of acknowledgment or compensation. I use "goodness" in the same sense as I would use the term "harmless." Metaphysics teaches there is no right and wrong or good and bad, for to think in such terms implies judgment. It does teach, however, of knowledge and ignorance, or harmlessness and harmfulness, each inexorably connected to the other. We act harmfully (sin) out of ignorance and knowledge gained from experience teaches us to be harmless. The only punishment incurred is the karma we have wrought upon ourselves, and the real devil is our own ego that acts out of ignorance, tempting us to behave in a manner not in keeping with divine or cosmic law.

Modern religion often uses the devil as a scapegoat, something to single out and blame for their own or their follower's shortcomings. In some religions, the devil is used to instill fear and to subjugate its churchgoing members into accepting its dictates and dogma. I believe that motivation by fear or guilt is essentially negative and does nothing to further our spiritual development. On the contrary, by surrendering to such thought, we inherently place ourselves in a position of low self-esteem, encouraging a poor self-image, lack of self-confidence and an overall feeling of unworthiness. Clouding our spiritual insight, it serves only to create a separation between ourselves and our soul.

The divine self, high self or soul, is our Christ center, a superconscious state that lies dormant (for the most part) within each of us. Our dreams attempt to help us gain entrance to this center, by moving us closer to our inner spiritual essence, showing us how to overcome the barriers of separation we have created. Constructed of doubt, fear, hatred, greed, prejudice and guilt, they are obstacles we must confront to remove. Each segment we remove allows us to further our integration a bit more. So step by step, increment by increment, we progress ever closer to our soul's desire.

A common barrier we erect is one born of insecurity— essentially afraid to love. Yet, if we gave our love unconditionally, without expectation or reservation, we would not feel insecure. Love is an energy in motion that cannot be controlled or secured. Its law is simple: what we dispense, is returned to us with interest. But because most of us cannot identify with an egoless type of love, we open ourselves up to heartbreak and pain. Dreams attempt to teach us how to love unconditionally by pointing out our self-centered interests. Unconditional love begins when we let go of trying to place or live up to any expectations. By discarding expectation, we totally eliminate disappointment from our lives.

Inner barriers produce outer walls, which we place between ourselves and others. The persona, for example, is a mask we wear because we are afraid to let others see us in our true light. Fearing another's judgment however, corresponds on a deeper level to our fear of God's judgment. If we knew wholeheartedly that when felt, God's unconditional love would move us to tears, we would not place such importance on another's opinion, only their need to express it. The highest motivating force is unconditional love, and when one abides within that force there can be no feelings of guilt and shame.

We learn through trial and error how to become harmless, and how to love. Since this is a path built from our mistakes, it is imperative we do not judge, condemn or criticize others for their mistakes. By doing so we deny them their right to spiritual growth. The first step in becoming harmless is to accept everyone just the way they are, without attempting to change them. After all, they have as much right to their faults as we have to ours.

The persona is our shield, our protection against harm and ridicule. Yet it causes us to face our deepest fear: loneliness. We cannot put walls around ourselves and not be lonely. We place ourselves in isolation, imprisoning our feelings and restricting our manner of expression to create the illusion of a person that does not exist. The dream will attempt to shatter that illusion in no uncertain terms. It points out to us what we do not want to see, and tells us what we do not want to hear.

Essentially, this is the spiritual side of dreaming, always attempting to lead us back to the light by way of truth. Every insight we make is considered growth, and each symbol that depicts growth is a spiritual one. Trees, flowers, and grass are spiritual symbols. So is the sky that reflects the heavens. A placid lake is a reflection of the soul and climbing a mountain symbolizes our struggle to reach greater heights. The ocean represents the vast ocean of truth and the inner depths of our being. Spiritual symbols strengthen our understanding, giving us a deeper sense of faith. For this reason, they often bring peace when reflected upon, and joy when experienced.

DREAM THERAPY

There are various types of dream therapy. Many involve the participation of the dreamer in group work such as dream psychodrama, dialoguing, dream art and the like. There are times, however, when the urgency of a case requires moving quickly to the issue to uncover a particular cause. Because the client is usually not trained in dreamwork, the responsibility falls squarely upon the shoulders of the analyst. We now have a dilemma that has caused some disagreement in the dream field. Because analysts of the different schools of psychology have their own thoughts about dreams, symbols and their meanings, we have a multitude of ideas, some of which clash. The result is that the dream becomes misinterpreted by an attempt to fit it into the analyst's way of thinking, a way in which he or she was trained to think. This in turn has caused a backlash among certain members of the field.

With considerable influence, they have created another school of thought stating that only the dreamer can accurately interpret his or her dream. In many respects this is true, especially when you have a therapist that has Jungian, Freudian or Behavioral tunnel vision. I know this from my own personal experience. However, to state that an interpretation of a dream from an outside source is always a projection of another onto the dreamer, manipulating and misleading the dreamer into believing something false, I feel is an overreaction. Some schools admittedly attempt to preserve the mystery of a dream, feeling that perhaps we were either not meant to know or are incapable of knowing everything about dreams.

Dreamwork is both an art and a science, and it is the nature of the artist to paint just as it is the instinct of a scientist to explore. Our progressive development demands we work in this manner. To discount interpretive methodology entirely is (if I am permitted to use an old cliche') akin to throwing the baby out with the bathwater.

A client of mine was dying of lung cancer. His doctors

had given him only three more months to live and he came to me seeking a spiritual healing. Because of the time factor, I felt we could not uncover the underlying cause of his illness by conventional methods quickly enough to treat it. I requested he return the following week and bring his dreams, writing each one out in as much detail as possible. He returned with three dreams. The first is as follows:

I was a rookie cop and my partner was much older, with a nicely cultivated mustache much like mine. My gun was a very small automatic with a big clip on the side and the bullets were much too big for the gun. The senior officer praised the gun, which I thought was rather odd. I left with my partner and another rookie and drove downtown. We passed a blond prostitute and my partner stopped the car, told me to go back and get propositioned, then arrest her. I approach her from behind, she turns around and is a man with a beard and mustache. Confused and embarrassed, I walk on by.

I rejoin my partner, who is creeping uphill on his hands and knees. He tells me we are to arrest a large group of people inside a courtyard. The people were mostly middle-aged and did not appear to be breaking any laws. The three of us tried to gather them all up but many just walked away. We fired into the air, making a loud noise. I'm not sure my gun is working, as a large spent shell is hung up in the barrel. I work it loose and follow a group of people upstairs to a hallway with many doors. Now they are all gone but two women, one young and one old. I force them to return to the main group, during which the young one struggles and falls down, exposing her body. I touch her private parts and when she complains I tell her not to worry, that I've seen it all before. I hope they will run away and somehow escape, but they follow me back down to the main group. My senior partner apologizes for not helping me. I notice his mustache again.

The first sentence tells me this man, who we will call John, is a novice in *policing* an issue. The *gun* symbolizing protection was very small. He is also using the *wrong ammunition.* Driving downtown they spot a *prostitute.* This key leaped out at me, and I knew it was crucial, because downtown is *where the action is*—which was, in this case, the cancer. Here, we discover a prostitute, meaning that John is either prostituting himself or is somehow involved with prostitutes, which directly relates to his cancer.

The dream is telling him that when he attempts to *arrest* the situation on a conscious level he passes right by it because it is *disguised* (the beard and mustache). In the meantime the cancer is creeping up on him. In a sweeping raid he hopes to catch all the contributing elements, yet many slip away. When he examines what he has, he really cannot find (isolate) any problem, although he is making a lot of noise about his situation. Going upstairs (to his mind) he finds *two women.* One exposes herself (reveals her meaning). The genitals usually refer to sex. *He was touching upon a sexual area.* He hopes they will depart, but instead, they follow him back to the main group or issue, indicating they are important symbols. His *partner* is of course himself, who never did leave the scene (hanging on to the cancer) and is apologizing for it.

I slowly raised my head from the paper before me. John's eyes looked questioningly into mine.

"John," I said, breaking a long silence. "The issue here is honesty, and you're literally dying to get it off your chest." A puzzled expression crossed his face as continued to stare at me. At this point I was unaware if the keyword, *prostitute,* was literal or symbolic. I simply said, "It has to do with prostitution." His eyes abruptly shifted downward, but not quickly enough for me miss their startled look. I knew I had hit home.

"Do you want to talk about it?" I asked. Slowly, he began

to tell me of a long-standing affair he had with a prostitute. In doing so, he broke the one promise his wife asked him to make. She said his being unfaithful was the only thing she could never forgive. Seeing in this a lesson for them both, I realized that the two women who were *upstairs* in his dream symbolized the two women in his life, about whom the issue revolved.

"She has no choice but to forgive you, John. Just as you have no choice but to tell her. The sooner you tell her, the quicker we can get started." Genuine fear shown in his eyes. After much pleading and asking for alternatives he began to accept his situation.

"You know," he said, "this is the hardest thing I've ever had to do in my life."

"It's not always easy to do the right thing." I sympathized. "But in this case, your life may depend on it. Which do you choose?"

While I was reading John's dream, I broadly sectioned it off. Where he first mentions the blond prostitute I wrote in the left-hand margin: "The key which can unravel." Alongside the section where he saw she had a beard and mustache, I wrote: "What's causing the cancer—deception." By the part where they were making the arrest, I put: "Wanting to arrest it." Where he saw the people weren't breaking any laws, I made the notation, "Can't find the problem." When they began to slip away, I wrote: "Can't get it all, some slips away."

I made my interpretation without the help of my guides as they long since felt that any further help on their part would lead to a dependency from me—although I would enlist and receive their aid in other areas, such as healing. The analysis was done entirely by interpretive methodology, beginning by sectioning the dream off, and later by underlining the keys and associating them. A dream always speaks to the dreamer in the dreamer's own language. (An auto mechanic in our dream class contributed most of the auto parts definitions found in the dictionary section.)

John was a trucker, and it was important for me to analyze this dream through the eyes of a trucker. Most importantly, John is a human being, susceptible to the mass conscious programming of right and wrong, good and bad. From infancy we are programmed that if you are bad you must be punished. John made a mistake, one he will surely learn and grow from, but his guilt and shame are causing him to endure a harsh and unnecessary punishment. It was imperative that his wife forgive him. This would open the door to his own self-forgiveness, allowing him to have a more receptive condition, open to healing.

Feeling he had enough for one day, I set the second dream aside to read at a later time, concluding the session by attempting to give him some encouragement. I felt strongly that this forty-two-year-old man with his life still before him, would be open to a healing. My enthusiasm however, was not met. Confronted with having to tell his wife created an additional burden. His shoulders slumped as I escorted him to the door. He came expecting a miracle, hoping to sweep his "sins" under the rug and receive a healing. Now he faced yet another challenge. I know a part of him felt he would rather die than let his wife know he had been unfaithful.

It wasn't until the following day that I had the opportunity to read John's second dream. When I found a quiet moment, I sat down, and this is what I read:

I'm driving a truck and have a friend behind me in another rig. I stop at a restaurant (my friend is no longer there) and climb out the passenger side, stepping over a dog house. As I leave I notice the driver's seat is a swivel chair with the back facing me. At a phone booth, I try to call my wife but the operator tells me my credit card is invalid. I have to convince him that we've paid our bill and he tries again, but there's still no answer.

In the cafe, the waitress holds up a Denver omelet that

I didn't order. I accept it and ask for a Denver sandwich and a French roll which I don't eat. I go outside and look up to the sky. I see a red '54 Ford panel truck towing a black '54 Chevy. They are falling at an angle and land in a lake to my right, followed by dozens of old cars in mint condition. Some land in a lake, others on the road. Those that come at me are easy to avoid. One, a blue GMC pickup, lands on the lake like a seaplane, floating on the surface. Others just crash and sink. I think the cars are empty, but then I see brake lights. One car has an ugly old man in it. I think maybe he's dead.

Now I'm with my wife and she wants me to get her red dress out of the closet. There are two red dresses and two sweaters on hangers. She wants me to put one hanger on each finger while removing one of her dresses. I can't do it that way so I just grab the dress she wants and hand it to her.

I then go outside to an elaborate rock garden and patio area. My neighbors see me, and I feel guilty and out of place. As I walk back to the house I see a yellow cat lying in the doorway. It's raining, but part of the cat is dry in a half circle area of his fur. I go back inside but I don't let the cat in since he's not mine. I tell my wife about the cars falling from the sky, telling her that they fell from the back door of a plane, although I really didn't know for sure.

If the symbols in this dream were gold, and I a miner, I would have thought I found the "mother lode." I will not attempt to deluge the reader with all I found, but encourage those so inclined to pursue their examination of this dream further. In brief, I saw that the dreamer did not wish to be in the *doghouse*, and his lack of communication with his wife was not to his *credit*. I interpreted the *Denver omelet* to be mixed feelings and the *French roll*, well, the prostitute's first name was French. I considered *red* to mean warning or danger and *black*—death. *Fifty-four* vibrates to a nine, symbolizing termination or ending and the *cars* represent other issues that he was avoiding. The *ugly old man* was an ugly old issue presumed dead, while a *closet* usually contains secrets.

The fact there were *two red dresses* concerned me. Were there two areas that needed to be "addressed?" Two issues contributing to the cancer? Two sweaters could symbolize two issues the dreamer was *sweating* over. In any case, he needed to put a *finger* on all of it, which he didn't do. The yellow cat on his doorstep was most significant. It symbolized his unconscious fears or cowardice: "What lies at your doorstep." His fear of disclosing the truth to his wife blocked his path. It could also be amplified to represent an archetypal figure that mystics call *the dweller on the threshold. Rain* often symbolizes tribulation: "Into each life a little rain must fall." The *semicircle,* half dry and half wet, indicates a half-truth. Being *all wet* often means being wrong or untruthful. By not allowing the cat to gain entrance, he was refusing to face his feelings on a conscious level. Telling his wife the cars fell from the *rear door* of the plane meant he was not being "up front" with her. A *plane* usually represents a higher plane or level of thought. Here, I believe it meant a more truthful level or the *plain* truth.

The third dream reiterated the messages of the other two— a different plot, yet the same basic theme. In general, I noticed the dreams were strongly yang, suggesting a need for the dreamer to develop his yin side further. I also believe there were indications that he bore some resentment toward women. He definitely was a "macho" male, who reportedly left a trail of broken hearts. There were certainly more questions that needed to be answered before I could truly be of help. My teachers taught that in order for a healing to be effective, we must first clear up the karma:

IT IS WITHIN THE LOWER ELEMENTS OF MAN'S

PSYCHE THAT PHYSICAL AILMENTS OFTEN ARISE. THESE ARE THE AILMENTS WITHIN MAN'S SECRET SELF, WHICH CANNOT BE ELIMINATED THROUGH MODERN MEDICINE. ALTHOUGH DRUGS CAN BRING ABOUT A CHEMICAL CHANGE IN THE PHYSICAL BODY, THE EFFECT WEARS OFF BECAUSE THE CAUSE REMAINS FESTERING WITHIN. THEREFORE, IN ORDER TO EFFECT A PERMANENT HEALING, THERE MUST BE AN EMOTIONAL CHANGE WITHIN THE PSYCHE.

DISEASE IS USUALLY THE RESULT OF WAR BETWEEN THE SOUL AND THE BODY. THE SOUL IS CONDITIONED BY LAWS OF THE HIGHER PLANES WHILE THE BODY IS THE VICTIM OF THE FORCES OF DESIRE POURING THROUGH THE LOWER ASPECTS OF THE MIND. THE BODY IS A VICTIM OF THE SUBCONSCIOUS MIND OPERATING THROUGH THE SYMPATHETIC NERVOUS SYSTEM, WHICH OPERATES AUTOMATICALLY THROUGH THE ETHERIC VEHICLE.

PSYCHOSOMATIC ILLNESS IS A DISEASE OF THE BODY CAUSED BY EMOTIONAL TENSION WITHIN THE MIND. DISEASE OF THIS NATURE IS USUALLY CREATED IN THE PRESENT LIFE AS A RESULT OF THE MIND'S INABILITY TO ADJUST TO PRESENT PROBLEMS.

ORGANIC ILLNESSES, FREQUENTLY RECOGNIZED AS BEING ROOTED IN KARMA, ARE OFTEN BROUGHT INTO INCARNATION FROM PAST LIVES. THE PULLING FORCE OF KARMA WILL NOT READILY LEND ITSELF TO ANY TYPE OF HEALING OF A PERMANENT NATURE. THE SYMPTOMS MAY BE TEMPORARILY ALLEVIATED THROUGH HEALING OF ONE TYPE OR

ANOTHER, BUT THE PHYSICAL PROBLEM WILL STILL REMAIN, EMERGING LATER, IN PERHAPS ANOTHER AREA OF THE BODY, AND POSSIBLY EVEN IN A DIFFERENT FORM. IF, HOWEVER, DURING THE COURSE OF THE ILLNESS THE KARMIC LESSON HAS BEEN LEARNED, THE BODY WILL RESPOND TO TREATMENT OF EITHER A PHYSICAL OR PSYCHIC NATURE, AND A HEALING WILL PREVAIL.

My thought was to have John do some detective work on himself by uncovering any other possible areas of guilt. I outlined a prayer of forgiveness for him to say after each soul-searching and prepared some visualization exercises. I knew ultimately it was John who had to forgive himself. Negative karma is essentially our own judgment, and there is no sterner judge than us, busily creating our karma right in our own minds. Because of this, I was prepared to do some hypnotic regression work in an attempt to uncover any repeating patterns or conditions possibly carried over from a past life.

After outlining a definite course, I was ready to give it my all, working with John to the extent he would allow. Arriving promptly for our next meeting, I was disappointed he did not bring any dreams, and even more disappointed to hear he had not told his wife. I sensed it alarmed him to discover his dreams were so revealing, and he felt somewhat embarrassed at disclosing so much at our last session. Directing my questions toward his health and present state of mind, I hoped to lead the conversation into something more substantial. When I mentioned how it might be a good idea to quit the beer and red meat, his face paled.

"I just came to that conclusion myself," he said with a shocked expression. "Are you somehow reading my mind?"

I briefly assured him that I wasn't, explaining that it was

a synchronous event and we probably both felt the importance of abstaining from those particular foods. I felt that John was becoming a little paranoid and resistant to further counseling. As it turned out, I was right. During that session I again explained the necessity for forgiveness and the importance of delving deeper to uncover any other underlying causes for his illness.

The religious ritual of confession and forgiveness utilizes spiritual and psychological principles. First we confess, admitting to ourselves we made a mistake. Second, we must be contrite, wishing never to repeat that particular mistake again. Third, we must accept penance, which would be doing some good work to compensate for our error. This balances the negative with a positive, and clears the path to forgiveness, resulting in a clean slate and allowing communion with the divine self within. John listened to all I said, but contributed little. He stated the doctors were optimistic about an operation that would remove half his lung and asked what my feelings were. I told him to follow his intuition, knowing he had already made up his mind. I gave him the prayer, visualization exercises, some relaxation tapes and reading material, instructing him once again to tell his wife.

Our third and last session was brief. He stated that he told his wife and her tumultuous reaction was almost more than he could bear. After a couple of trying days of exchanges, where she went through a complete emotional cycle, she finally accepted his apology, and to the best of my knowledge forgave him. It was a touching moment, which he stated brought them closer together than they had ever been before. John never kept his last appointment as he was preparing for a lengthy stay at the hospital. He called, stating that the operation was scheduled in three days and he was to be admitted the following day. In our phone conversation I wished him well and promised I would pray for him.

John lived for fifteen more months, during which he received chemotherapy treatments, never giving up hope until the very end. A devoted husband and father, he was given the opportunity to learn love in the fullest sense of the word, and I believe he did. He did it his way, a way that was not necessarily right or wrong, simply a way that he selected. Everything is by choice and having his own reasons, John chose to go at that time and in that particular fashion.

EGO TRANSCENDENCE

Dreams encourage us to change, but if we are unaware of the benefits involved, we will be less inclined to make the necessary effort. This creates a demand for those working within the dream field to focus upon support, encouraging the dreamer to make the necessary changes by emphasizing both the tangible and intangible benefits—ultimately striving to bring the dreamer to greater heights through self-realization. We are all headed in the same direction regardless of which path we choose, and we all have a common goal: to transcend our ego. Buddha did it while sitting under the Bodhi tree. Jesus did it in forty days and nights spent in the desert. Many spiritual disciples devote their entire lives to this task. Difficult as it may appear, it is within our grasp, and no greater help can be found than that supplied by our dreams. All that remains is for us to make a study of the ego using the obvious firsthand example of self.

Psychology is the philosophy and science of mind and behavior. It includes the analysis and evaluation of the individuality and the manner of its expression. Its purpose is to heal the mind, therefore proposing a study of human consciousness. It has branched out into several distinct schools of thought, some of which take into consideration the spiritual nature of the individual, while others consider the mind to be a source of a person's psychological makeup, rather than simply the mechanism for its expression. This view gives one the impression that the personality is more or less self-contained, with external influences being the sole factors affecting its behavior. The personality is then treated as the center of consciousness with the aim of bringing it into line with accepted standards of normalcy.

While these standards may vary somewhat from school to school they generally accept that fear of death (the unknown) is a basic part of our nature, linked to a self-preservation instinct. Also commonly accepted is the desire for wealth beyond that necessary to supply and maintain our basic needs. Success is equated with status and authority, so it is perfectly *normal* to be envious and resentful, to become angry and have one's feelings hurt. "Such is the nature of man" it is argued, and not without a measurable amount of truth. It therefore appears normal for us to be insecure to one degree or another, since all the above attitudes are motivated by insecurity. If this is so, then the mass consciousness of humanity is unstable and will remain unstable until the prime motivating force (fear) is replaced with the proper motivating force of love.

The average individual, usually caught up in a struggle between the two, creates a framework of conflicts, struggling with the dichotomy of right and wrong or good and bad. In the process the belief structure is constantly being altered to accommodate bits and pieces of information assimilated through experience. Metaphysics teaches that the purpose of life is the evolution of consciousness through experience and expression, and that all life is contained by purpose within a grand scheme of cyclic evolution. Progress, measured by one's ability to work through these levels of consciousness, is symbolically depicted as an upward climb or struggle. If we study our dream content while keeping this in mind, we find the most valuable tool for self-growth imaginable.

The conscious mind or waking consciousness has a wide range of relative states of consciousness. The undeveloped, unevolved or undisciplined mind often works on an instinctual, subconscious, or self-centered level. The more highly evolved mind works more on an intuitive, detached level in close alignment with the soul. When the waking consciousness functions in rapport with the soul, a significantly different quality of consciousness emerges. In this quality of consciousness there is no fear of death and no insecurity. Instead, there is a basic need to contribute to humanity with no egoic tendency toward recognition and little desire for self-indulgence.

Success is measured by a different yardstick from the average and would therefore not be within the "accepted" range of normalcy as commonly viewed today. Richard Bucke spoke of "cosmic consciousness" in his book by the same title. Abraham Maslow mentions "self-actualized" individuals who are motivated by the higher good, and Jung mentions individuation: "the conscious coming to terms with one's own inner center," resulting in maturation or growth.[1]

Jung presented a psychology with metaphysical overtones that reached deep into man's psyche. Exploring the meaning of dreams and symbols, he contributed greatly in that area. Unfortunately, he saw the *collective unconscious* as primarily a habitat for *archetypes* and viewed its influence upon mankind from that perspective, rather than pursuing the effect of thoughtforms as presently generated by mass consciousness, which greatly affects humanity as a whole. He clearly saw there are both concrete and abstract levels of the mind. His belief was that symbols found on the abstract level (collective unconscious) influenced the ego (consciousness) to integrate certain separations of the self. It was this integrating tendency within the collective unconscious expressing itself as an archetype that represented the ego's potential wholeness which he called the "self."

While to some degree this may appear to parallel metaphysical thought, his conclusion was that *consciousness cannot exist without an ego*. This is in direct contrast to metaphysical philosophy that views the ego as a product of the self, expressed as the driving force of the personality necessary to carry it to a certain point in consciousness before being transcended. This transcendence takes place when the personality identifies with the soul as the true self rather than the ego, thus completing integration. Once complete, the personality becomes the willing instrument of the soul, motivated by spiritual consciousness.

Three principal schools of thought are generally acknowledged in psychology: Behavioral, Humanistic and Psychoanalytic. Maslow took a holistic approach in which he claimed to incorporate these three methods into a fourth, which he called "Transcendence." He stated that those motivated by higher levels of consciousness are:

> Self-actualized individuals (more mature, more fully human), by definition already suitably gratified in their basic needs, are now motivated in other higher ways, to be called "metamotivators."[2]

Maslow was considered to be a pioneer in the field of emerging "value-seeking psychology," and was held in high esteem by Roberto Assagioli, who systematically used all the available techniques, claiming "Psychosynthesis" can be applied by the individual to foster and accelerate inner growth and self-actualization.[3] Acknowledging a permanent center beyond the ego, he does not equate it directly to the soul or superconscious, feeling that superconsciousness is separate and distinct from the consciousness attained through self-realization. Metaphysical philosophy maintains there are three lower centers of consciousness (chakras).[4] These lower states parallel those of Freud's "id," the primitive, infantile aspect of the ego whose seat is found in the libido. Both agree that these states are founded in insecurity, but metaphysics teaches they can be overcome through enlightenment, allowing the individual to progress to higher centers of consciousness.

Jung uses the term *ego* as more or less synonymous with normal waking consciousness while in Freud's terminology the ego has both conscious and unconscious components. Modern psychology has expanded the term broadly and in the process it has become less defined. It appears that the humanist psychologists are trying to expand it to cover the higher levels of consciousness as well. It is difficult for traditional psychology to believe that after a certain level of consciousness is attained, *I-ness* ceases to exist in place of *we-ness*. Rarely do my guides speak in terms of "I" or "me." I found this to be true in other cases of ego transcendence as well. Since they are all of One Mind which is in accord with Itself, they speak unanimously.

In the metaphysical sense, the ego is perceived as an aspect of the personality, choosing to express itself through the lower centers of consciousness. By degrees, in learning how to let go (detachment), and to love unconditionally, we progress to sixth center (Christ) consciousness, and it is here the ego is transcended. In that center a shift in identity takes place that causes the self to be observed as a part of the whole around whom all parts revolve. The ego considers itself to be the whole, around which everything revolves; a deluded consciousness motivated by self-centered experience and expression. When it is finally shed, a spiritual transformation takes place and motivation is supplied from a different (spiritual) source. The ego can be more properly defined as the relatively conscious part of the personality that relates directly with the external reality via sense impression on a physical, mental and emotional level. This external reality is based upon the false premise of physical existence being separate from the spiritual. The illusion is that physical existence is all there is, being complete and self-fulfilling within itself. It offers glamour, romance and excitement. But without the spiritual, it becomes a hollow facade behind which nothing exists.

The soul has one set of values and the ego another. The soul recognizes its immortal perfection while the ego cannot see beyond its own limitations. When the personality shares the same set of values as the soul it is said to be expressing higher consciousness. Since the average person vacillates between the two, they create needed conflicts, which serve to resolve key differences and restore balance. The personality creates its own experiences (problems) in order to find the solution. The solution, however, may only be found at a higher level of consciousness, forcing the individual to shift (grow) to that level in order to resolve the problem. When misled by ego consciousness there is a tendency to blame external conditions, situations or events for any unhappiness, while refusing to accept responsibility for self-created problems.

The perspective provided by the mainstream of modern psychology does not comfortably accommodate a comprehensive theory of growth, nor does it clarify what instigates the motivating force for personal development. It also does not provide the answer as to how the ego can be transcended. As long as it chooses to ignore these fundamental issues and not view the personality as a mechanism through which the human soul can be expressed as the very essence of a person's being, it remains in a sense, quite limited.

There are a growing number of individuals within this profession, however, who are taking into account the influence and wisdom of the soul, the experience gained from past lives, race mind influence, information received from other planes, possession by discarnate entities, and the help we receive from our guides. Previously all such influences were relegated to one's unconscious or the collective unconscious, where they have been narrowly perceived as mysterious "paranormal forces" or an emergence from one's "dark side."

Many in the transpersonal movement recognize that ego transcendence results in spiritual growth, and the dawn of a new psycho-spiritual era is upon us. Segments of humanity are now awakening and a transition is taking place in mass consciousness. The combined knowledge of psychology and spirituality provide a formidable tool in assisting with this transformation.

Ego transcendence is the single most important benefit derived from dreamwork, as it is always accompanied by an increase in consciousness. Any expansion of consciousness is marked by a comparable decrease of the unconscious, automatically opening up the individual to more meaningful and profound dreams. Once the superconscious is aware of the seriousness of one's efforts toward self-development or spiritual growth, it gently guides and aids the seeker in furthering that growth. Soon, a line of communication between the personality and the soul is established, and when this occurs, it will be found to be in the language of dreams.

Dream Dictionary

HOW TO USE THIS DICTIONARY

The definitions in this dictionary have all been compiled from actual dreams. The majority were submitted by students of my workshops and classes. Some were borrowed from Edgar Cayce. My wife Michelle and I contributed a fair amount from our personal dream journals. A few were also contributed by our dream guides. The main point to remember is **A DREAM SYMBOL DOES NOT HAVE A FIXED MEANING.** This is why in some cases you will find two or more dissimilar definitions for the same symbol. It indicates some dreamers found different meanings. In many instances, one readily can see a more obvious symbolic definition than presently given. The reason such an alternative may be lacking is because no one submitted a dream with that particular meaning for the symbol.

Our language, customs and attitudes are always changing, and the flexible language of symbols responds in kind. Colloquial and slang expressions of yesterday and their symbology are now, for the most part, obsolete. I doubt for instance, that anyone refers to eyes as "peepers" anymore, or a gun as a "rod." When was the last time you heard the expression "I've been hoodwinked?" By the same token, I doubt that in those days dreaming of drinking a particular type of cola would symbolize taking cocaine, or mowing a lawn would represent a dream message to cut out the "grass" or marijuana. Also, every dream dictionary that I have read has politely omitted symbols stemming from the common vernacular. Yet, privately, this is how many of us think. Colloquialism plays a strong role in every language and dreams are no exception.

This dictionary is meant to give the reader examples of dream symbols from actual dreams so they can get a better understanding of just how the dream mind operates. It can help by giving the dreamer a point of reference from which to start. In studying a symbol one can move correspondingly to another symbol through association. When we actually see how other people associate their symbols, it may give us an inkling as to where to begin. So if nothing else, it could add a few drops of oil to the interpreter's mental gears. Lastly, I included this dictionary so that students and professionals alike can appreciate the candor, humor and creativity of the dream-producing mind.

A

ABDOMEN: the third chakra (emotional seat). 2. Gut feelings or gut level.

ABORTION: aborting a plan or idea. 2. Denying an expression of life.

ACCIDENT: a clash of thoughts, plans, ideas or personalities.

ACID: a possible physical condition. 2. Sour manner or disposition.

ACTOR: act or role one assumes. 2. Portrayal of an attitude assumed by the dreamer.

ADDRESS: what the dreamer is addressing.

ADMIRAL (NAVY): personification of worthiness; an admirable act or trait.

ADVERTISEMENT: revealing certain things about oneself or others.

AFRICA: unconscious or subconscious mind.

AFTERNOON: drawing to a close, nearing the end.

AIRLINE FLIGHT (DEPARTURE): running away, escaping. **(ARRIVAL):** materialization of goals.

AIRPLANE: an elevated plane of thought (high ideas). 2. Astral projection. 3. Taking "flight."

AIRPORT: plans or ideas either "taking off" or coming into being.

ALARM CLOCK: the ringing of an alarm clock signifies a warning. 2. An alarming event or situation.

ALLEY: a passage in the mind. 2. If dark, the unconscious.

ALTAR: what the dreamer worships. 2. If sacrificial, a sacrifice the dreamer is making.

AMBASSADOR: liaison between the conscious and unconscious minds.

AMBULANCE: warning of impending illness. 2. An emergency situation.

ANIMALS: Animals usually represent their particular traits or characteristics. See the following listings.

   ALLIGATOR: fears. Vicious or destructive speech.

   APE: to imitate. See Monkey.

   ARMADILLO: having a "hard" exterior. 2. Armor or protection.

   BAT: nocturnal activities. 2. "Blind as a bat."

   BEAR: a difficult situation—"It's a bear." 2. Overbearing.

   BEAVER: industrous, hardworking; "busy as a beaver."

   BIRD: freedom or free spirit. 2. One's ability to "fly" or "soar."

   BUFFALO: being misled or "buffaloed."

   BULL: stubborn or "bullheaded." 2. Bullying or intimidating. See Astrological Signs.

   CROW: negative elements or influences. 2. A raven symbolizes death.

   CAT: a yin attribute, often the unconscious. 2. If a family pet, it may represent a trait or characteristic of the dreamer.

   CHICKEN: fearfulness.

   COW: an overweight or pregnant female.

   DEER: a play on words for dear. 2. A timid or gentle female. 3. A buck represents an attractive male. 4. A stag represents a "single" male or one who is going "stag."

   DOG: an unattractive person. 2. Companion, guide or protector. 3. Playfulness. 4. If threatening: bad temperament.   5. Something that's "dogging" the dreamer.

ELEPHANT: the subconscious mind.   2. Strength of mind, character or ideals.   3. Memory.

FOX: cleverness, to "outfox."

GIRAFFE: as seen from a "higher perspective."

GOAT: irked; "getting your goat."   2. "An old goat." See Astrological Signs.

GUINEA PIG: being played upon or experimented with.

HORSE: freedom.   2. One's ability to eat.

LAMB: innocence.   2. Spirituality or Christ presence.

LION: anger or aggressive behavior, often one's mate or lover. See Astrological Signs.

MONKEY: mischieviousness; "monkey business" or "monkeying around." Usually concerning something not in the dreamer's best interests.

MOUSE: lack of assertiveness or self-confidence; timidity.

MULE: a "work" animal, feeling overworked. 2. Stubbornness.

OCTOPUS: hanging or clinging onto something.

OPPOSUM: pretending; "playing 'possum."

OWL: wisdom.   2. Late night activities; "night owl."

OXEN: a cart being drawn by oxen pertains to strength in carrying one's load or burden. An ox symbolizes the dreamer's strength.

PARROT: to mimic or "parrot" someone else.

PIG: to overindulge.   2. Overweight.   3. Eating pork.

RABBIT: quick or fleeting.   2. A high degree of sexual activity.

RAT: a treacherous individual.

ROOSTER: a prideful male.

SHEEP: to follow or be led by someone else. 2. The masses. Stray sheep are thoughts gone astray.

SKUNK: an untrustworthy individual. 2. Zero; to get "skunked."

SNAKE: sexual desire or drive. 2. The kundalini energy or creative force. 3. A negative individual such as "a snake in the grass."

SQUIRREL: to hide, store or "squirrel away." 2. A "squirrely looking" person.

TURTLE OR TORTOISE: moving slowly or cautiously. 2. Feeling protected.

WHALE: a large issue.

ANTIQUE: antiquated or outdated ideas. 2. Old feelings.

APARTMENT: an isolated aspect of oneself. 2. A contributing factor to the whole or complete situation.

APPLAUSE: approval, encouragement or support.

APPLE: tempting or appealing.

APPLIANCE: application; either needed or being directed to a given area.

APPOINTMENT: a point being made.

APRON: domesticity. 2. Dependence, such as being "tied to mother's apron strings."

AQUARIUM: the mind; a "think tank." The fish represent one's thoughts.

ARCHAEOLOGICAL ARTIFACTS: uncovering old feelings or desires. If valuable, they may represent values, strengths or attributes.

ARGUMENT: a conflict within oneself.

ARM: an extension or branch of the self; the right arm symbolizes strength, power or the yang, while the left arm is symbolic of weakness, negativity or the yin.

ARMOR: protective cover, defenses, the persona.

ARMY: antibodies or immune system. 2. Aspects of self united to fight. 3. Play on words: "are me."

ARREST: to quit or cease. 2. To prevent.

ARROW: a straightforward message.

ART: depicting a talent of the dreamer.

ASHES: finished, reduced or consumed.

ASLEEP: to dream of someone asleep signifies being unconscious of what is going on; "asleep to the fact" or "asleep at the switch."

ASPHALT (PAVEMENT): "paving the way."

ASSASSINATE: to sabotage or destroy.

ASTROLOGICAL SIGNS: signs of the zodiac indicate either an individual born under that sign or something significant that may occur during that time period. Symbols for these signs are as follows: **Aries:** Ram, March 21 to April 20. **Taurus:** Bull, April 21 to May 21. **Gemini:** Twins, May 22 to June 21. **Cancer:** Crab, June 22 to July 22. **Leo:** Lion, July 23 to August 23. **Virgo:** Virgin, August 24 to September 23. **Libra:** Scales, September 24 to October 23. **Scorpio:** Scorpion, October 24 to November 22. **Sagittarius:** Archer, November 23 to December 21. **Capricorn:** Goat, December 22 to January 20. **Aquarius:** Water or Waterbearer, January 21 to February 19. **Pisces:** Fish, February 20 to March 20

ATTIC: see House.

AUSTRALIA: inner thoughts or feelings, which are found

"down under."

AUTOMOBILE: An automobile usually signifies the persona or self, although it can often represent the physical body and its parts or functions:

BATTERY: energy.

BRAKES: one's ability to stop or quit.

CARBURETOR: respiratory system.

CLUTCH: hanging on to something.

DISTRIBUTOR: distribution of energy.

DRIVER: control; "sitting in the driver's seat."

FAN: cooling off.

FRONT SEAT: conscious awareness.

FUEL: mental or physical diet.

FUEL PUMP: the heart.

GAUGES: gauging or monitoring something. 2. An indication being pointed out to the dreamer.

GEARS: the mind.

HEADLIGHTS: vision; the dreamer's perception.

IGNITION: starting up or starting power.

PASSENGER: a passive aspect. 2. Being "driven" to do something. 3. Being "taken for a ride."

RADIATOR: pressure.

REAR SEAT: beyond the dreamer's control. 2. Passiveness, "taking a back seat" to something.

SPARK PLUGS: pep, energy.

STEERING WHEEL: control. 2. A direction in which one is being "steered."

TAILLIGHT: warning to slow down.

TIRES: the energy one is "riding on."

TRUCK: a "work" vehicle; the working aspect of the dreamer.

WATER PUMP: circulation.

WHEELS: balance or footing.

WINDSHIELD: ability to see where one is going.

WIRING: nervous system, tension.

AX: "an ax to grind."   2. Being given "the ax."   3. To cut loose or get rid of.

B

BABY: an idea or plan in the developmental stage.   2. A developing aspect of the dreamer.   3. If it is one's own child it may signify a budding or newly developed creation by the parents.

BACK: the back is symbolic of support.   2. The burdens we carry.   3. Walking backward is taking a step back or stepping back in favor of someone or something else.

BAG: occupation.   2. The thoughts or feelings one carries around.

BALDNESS: thoughtlessness, not using the mind.   2. May also indicate hair loss or fear of same.

BANANA: a dietary message.   2. Phallic symbol.

BANK: what one is banking on.   2. Storehouse of inner or spiritual wealth.

BAPTISM: indoctrination.   2. Christening or awakening.

BARTENDER: attending to someone or something.

BATTERY: see Automobile.

BATHROOM: see House.

BEACH: the edge of the subconscious; a point where the conscious and unconscious meet.   2. Vacation or leisure time.

BEANS: something of little value.

BEARD: outward growth.   2. Maturity.

BED: a situation one has created for oneself.   2. Support or rest.

BELLS: heralding an important event in the life of the dreamer.

BELT: having to do with one's weight or diet.   2. Financial condition.

BICYCLE: balance or balancing.   2. Riding out a cycle.

BIRTHDAY: pregnancy.

BLANKET: concealment.   2. Security.

BLINDNESS: what the dreamer has lost sight of.

BLOOD: energy, vitality or life force.   2. Kundalini.

BOAT: a ship represents the voyage through life.   2. A small boat represents a particular issue in the dreamer's life. 3. Passing up an opportunity, "missing the boat." See Ship.

BOMB: a surprise, "dropping a bomb."   2. An unexploded bomb is a dud, as in "it's a bomb," or "bombing out."

BONES: inner exposure; "bare bones."

BOOK: knowledge.

BORDER: (GEOGRAPHICAL): inner boundaries of values or morals.

BOWEL MOVEMENT: eliminating something of a yang nature. See Toilet and/or Feces.

BOX: confinement or restriction; feeling "boxed in." See Container.

BRAIN: intelligence.

BRASSIERE: support.

BREAD: life.   2. Nourishment.   3. Financial support.

BRIDGE: connection.   2. Crossing over to another point of view.

BULLETS: verbal ammunition.

BUS: transporting or moving to a particular destination, usually of a subconscious nature.

C

CAKE: Fortelling of a wedding or birth.   2. Easy, such as "a piece of cake."

CAMERA: "picturing" oneself or others in a given situation.

CAN: to stop or contain.   2. Suppresed ideas or feelings.

CANCER: malignant thoughts.

CANDY: sexual feelings or desires.

CANTALOUPE: play on words, "can't elope."

CAST (characters): figures portraying aspects of the dreamer.   2. A plaster cast symbolizes a confining mold.

CASTLE: defensiveness.   2. Fantasy.   3. The home.

CAVE: primal feelings.   2. Security.

CAVEMAN: primitive mentality or attributes.

CELEBRITY: a well-known trait or attribute of the dreamer.

CEMETERY: buried or dead issues. See Grave.

CHAIN: strength.   2. Something binding or restricting.

CHILD: a developing aspect.   2. One's own child represents a joint issue, a creation of its parents.

CHILDREN: immature behavior. 2. Play.

CHURCH: a structured religious belief.

CLIENT: professional or vocational aspect.

CLOCK: the stilled hands of a clock mean that time has run out. 2. To clock or time something. 3. To measure in terms of time.

CLOSET: secret or hidden feelings.

CLOTHING: material feelings or persona. 2. Inappropriate or ill-fitting clothes may mean the dreamer is "ill-suited." Leisure wear symbolizes relaxation or time away from work. Business clothes represent the business persona, work clothes signify working aspect, etc.

COAT: protection, usually represents mentally or emotionally insulating oneself.

COLA (a popular brand): cocaine.

COINS: lots of coins indicate many changes, while a few, indicate small change. Large denominations indicate big change while gold coins indicate spiritual wealth or growth.

COLORS: Colors usually indicate moods or feelings. It is significant when one remembers a particular color in a dream.

> **BLACK:** a color of inactivity, stagnation and death. Symbolizes that which is hidden. Keywords are: negativity, concealment, repression and dark forces. Black may also indicate being "in the black" financially or on the books. If in combination with white it may mean "in black and white." Sexy black undergarments or black high-heel shoes have to do with sexual activity.

> **BLUE:** on one level it symbolizes motherhood, spirituality, integrity and idealism. On another level it describes the sea and the sky and in that sense is associated with freedom. It may also indicate sadness, as in "feeling blue."

BROWN: an earth color, possibly indicating "down to earth." Brown also symbolizes acquisitiveness and when mixed with other colors can denote selfishness.

GOLD: a color of expansion, it symbolizes wealth, spiritual wisdom and power.

GREEN: is associated with life, the planet, spring and growth. It is a color of healing and teaching. It is also a symbol of the "go" sign or "green light" indicating to move ahead. A yellowish-green denotes envy. Many times it represents money.

GRAY: mental activity, "gray matter" of the brain. Sadness and depression are also an aspect of this color. An area not clearly defined, as in "a gray area."

INDIGO: the bridge between the finite and the infinite. A high spiritual color symbolizing introspection and the "third eye."

ORANGE: associated with sunshine and vitality, it can indicate one's energy level. It is also a color of discrimination, harmony and wisdom.

PINK: warm tones are symbolic of spirituality, love and affection while colder tones indicate immaturity or infancy. It most commonly characterizes health, such as "in the pink."

PURPLE: nobility, dominion, power and authority are the keywords for this color. It denotes a sense of dedication, initiation, sacred rites and healing.

RED: a color of activity, challenge and adventure, it can also be a sign of excess. Primarily used as a warning or danger signal, it may denote courage, anger or sexual activity. Physically, it may represent the blood or blood cells.

WHITE: is the color of purity and cleanliness. Keywords are embracing, revealing, dynamic and stimulating. White light represents a higher or spiritual intelligence. In its purest sense it signifies illumination.

YELLOW: symbolizes the intellect. When depicted in the form of the sun's rays it is a guiding light. A pale or stark form of yellow can indicate cowardice.

COMICS: a humorous issue.

CONCRETE: solid or sound idea or foundation. 2. The concrete mental. 3. Stubborn or unyielding.

CONTAINER: A box, can or drum signifies what is contained within oneself; usually repressed feelings.

COOKING: planning or "cooking up" something.

CORD: connection, what one is "tied" to or "tied up" with.

CORRAL: to contain or keep "fenced in."

COUPLE: two people of the opposite sex signify a relationship. On another level the relationship is with oneself and symbolizes a balance or imbalance between the yin and yang.

COURTHOUSE: courtship and marriage.

COVERS: hiding or covering something up.

CRAB: bad temperament. See Astrological Signs.

CREDIT CARD: acknowledgment; giving or taking credit for something.

CROWD: a multiplicity of self. 2. Feeling crowded in or out. 3. Concerning the public, or something being made public.

CRYING: troubled, or warning of trouble.

CUP: knowledge. 2. Receptivity or the vessel of the self.

CURB: standing on a curb about to cross a street signifies making a decision. 2. Waiting for the traffic to pass means waiting for the right opportunity. 3. Controlling or suppressing.

D

DAGGER: sharp words.

DAM: holding back, pent-up emotions.

DANCING: happiness.   2. Romance.

DARTS: pointed words.

DAWN: new awareness.   2. Something that is forthcoming.

DAY: conscious awareness.   2. The present.

DEATH: transformation.   2. Termination or ending.

DEAFNESS: unheeding, "turning a deaf ear."

DEFECATE: in the toilet symbolizes elimination or purging, but upon someone or something is to sully.

DEFORMITY: malformed thoughts.

DEN: to examine or study.

DEPARTMENT STORE: a department within oneself.

DEPOT: departure or change; usually in thought or attitude.

DESERT: barren or empty.   2. Devoid of fulfillment.

DESPAIR: wrongdoing or feeling wronged.

DEVIL: feeling tormented.

DICE: a risky decision.   2. Putting something into motion that cannot be reversed. See Gambling.

DIGGING: uncovering something hidden or "buried" within oneself.

DINE: see Eat

DINING ROOM: the absorbing aspect of oneself.

DINOSAUR: something old or no longer in demand. 2. Feeling ancient.

DOLL: an unrealistic perception of another; not the true or real person, but a projection of the dreamer.

DOOR: see House.

DOWNHILL: worsening.

DRAGON: sexual energy.

DRESSED UP: presenting a favorable image.

DRIVING: a direction the dreamer is taking.

DROWNING: over-involvement; something the dreamer is "immersed" in to the extent that he or she is "in over their head."

DRUGS: see Medication.

DUMP: a garbage dump can represent the dreamer feeling "down in the dumps." 2. A message to get rid of something.

DUSK: the end of a cycle; "the curtain is drawn."

E

EARS: attention or inattention; something the dreamer needs to hear.

EAR PIERCING: having one's ears pierced means the dreamer has heard something which has "pierced" through to deeper levels of one's being.

EARTH: pertaining to physical matters or the physical body. 2. Nurturance or fertility.

EARTHQUAKE: emotional upheaval; getting "rattled" or "shook up."

EAT: to assimilate, ingest or absorb. It can relate to either a physical or mental diet.

ECHO: echoing one's thoughts or sentiments.

EEL: slippery thoughts.

EGGS: plans or ideas. Scrambled: jumbled up. Runny: incomplete or not "firmed up." Hard-boiled: hardened feelings.

EJACULATE: planting a seed of thought.

ELDERLY PEOPLE: old habits or patterns. See Oldsters.

ELEVATOR: a direction of the mind. Going up represents elevating one's thoughts or taking a higher viewpoint whereas going down signifies the reverse. Going down may also represent delving into the unconscious.

EMPLOYEE or EMPLOYER: work or job-related situation.

ENGLAND: the "mother country," an area where the dreamer's feelings and ideas are rooted.

ESTATE: a state of mind or being.

EUROPE: "you're up," a focus on oneself.

EXPENSE: the price one must pay; a cost to oneself.

EXPENSIVE: a high price to pay.

EXPLOSION: to vent one's anger. 2. Goofing up by "blowing it."

EYES: perception or insight.

EXCREMENT: see Feces.

F

FACE: what one is facing or needs to face. 2. How the dreamer presents him or herself. 3. A direction the dreamer is facing.

FAIR: an affair.

FAN: see Automobile.

FALLING: failing, or fear of failing in a given area of one's life, including health. 2. Falling into something, money, a job or a predicament.   3. The astral body re-entering the physical.

FAT: financially "well-padded."   2. A weight problem.

FATHER: intellect.   2. Dominant male aspect or parental advisor.   3. What the dreamer is "fathering."

FAUCET: feelings or emotions being turned on or off.

FECES: a symbol usually associated with the common vernacular. "Crap" or worthless material: "a bunch of shit." Lies: "pile of shit." Drunk: "shit-faced." Treated badly: "shit on," etc. See Toilet.

FEET: foundation.   2. Understanding.   3. Standing up for oneself.   4. Taking a stand.

FENCE: division, barrier or limitation.   2. If fallen down, it means the dreamer's defenses are down.   3. Indecision, if one is sitting on a fence.   4. To take offense.

FIGHTING: inner conflict.   2. Combating an illness.

FINGERS: to "put a finger on it." Index finger: pointing out something. Snapping fingers: message to pay attention.

FIRE: inflammatory, anger.   2. Passion.   3. Transformation. Smoldering embers indicate resentment. The aftermath of a fire symbolizes being exhausted or fed up: feeling "burned out."

FIRE ENGINE: warning that something is out of control.

FISH: ideas, thoughts, aspirations or goals. A hooked fish means attainment.

FISHING: what the dreamer is seeking or trying to "catch."

FISHING LINE: having "a line out," hoping to "land" something.

FIST: anger. An upraised fist indicates power.

FLAME: a flaming object indicates consuming passion. A

solitary flame such as a candle, matchstick, torch, etc. signifies a love relationship.

FLOATING: floating in the air is indecisiveness; "up in the air."

FLOOD: to become inundated; overwhelmed.

FLOWERPOT: marijuana.

FLOWERS: romance, love, friendship and happiness.   2. The spring season.   3. Blooming from spiritual growth.

FLY: pesty or bothersome.

FLYING: feeling uplifted or "high."   2. To rise above. 3. Astral projection.

FOIL: to wrap up in foil is to conceal something in an attempt to disrupt or "foil" one's plans.

FOOD: stimulation or "food for thought."   2. Information. May also signify nutritional needs.

FOREIGN COUNTRY: a distant or unfamiliar part of the dreamer.

FOREIGNER: an unfamiliar aspect of the dreamer.

FOREST: The mind. If dark, the unconscious.

FORK: a fork in a road signifies making a choice of some magnitude. The utensil indicates pickiness or picking out. 2. To "fork over" or "fork out."

FORT: defensiveness.

FREEWAY: a clear path.   2. Living a fast life.

FRIENDS: supportive aspects.

FROST: a cold atmosphere created between the dreamer and someone else.

FRUIT: coming to fruition.   2. The "fruit" of one's labors.

G

GAMBLING: taking a chance. If a winner, making a good choice.

GARBAGE: unproductive; waste.   2. Nonsense.

GARBAGE CAN: garbage the dreamer is harboring.

GARDEN: what the dreamer is cultivating.

GAS: intestinal disorder.

GASOLINE: energy; fuel for the body or mind.

GASOLINE FUMES: warning of breathing polluted air.

GATE: entryway to the mind. Closed indicates a "closed mind."

GAUGES: see Automobile.

GENITAL ORGANS: sexual activity or inactivity. If devoid of pubic hair: sexual immaturity. To touch, or observe someone's genitals being touched, can signify touching upon a private, sensitive or stimulating area.

GERMANS: germs.

GLASS: if clear, to view clearly.   2. Obscure: unclear perception.   3. Broken: shattered hopes.

GHOST: what is haunting the dreamer.

GOLD: something of value to the dreamer's well-being. 2. Higher wisdom or spiritual growth.

GOLDFISH: wise or valuable thoughts and ideas.

GRAVE: something "dead and buried."   2. A grave issue. A corpse or ghost coming out of a grave signifies something being revived or brought back to life.

GREEK: difficulty in comprehension, "it's all Greek to me."

GROCERY STORE: the dreamer's storehouse of thoughts and

feelings. Purchasing items can mean "buying" into those feelings.

GUN: to assail or protect, depending upon the context of the dream. See Shoot.

H

HAIR: outward growth. On the head: thoughts, or one's state of mind. The color and type of hair indicate type of thought. Red hair: anger, curly hair: hair-curling thoughts, black hair (if not one's natural color): negative thoughts. Haircut: a different, usually more positive way of thinking.

HALL: a large concert hall or theater concerns one's performance in life.

HAMMER: willfulness or driving force.

HAMMERING NAILS: to secure or make fast.

HANDS: to grasp or understand.   2. Holding onto.   3. To hand out or be handed something.   4. Handling a situation or one's feelings. The right hand is yang (positive), while the left relates to the yin (negative).

HAT: a *pre*occupation of the mind, *i.e.*, a fireman's hat: fiery thoughts, policeman's hat: arresting thoughts, etc.

HEAD: to lead or direct.   2. Intellect.

HEART: concerns matters of the heart. To feel another's heart through their chest indicates the dreamer's heart has been "touched."   2. The core or "heart" of a matter.

HEM: to hem, or anything having to do with one's hemline represents feelings of being "hemmed in."

HIGH SCHOOL: see School.

HILL: going uphill means proceeding under difficulty or laboriously. Downhill could mean regressing; "going downhill."

HINGE: vacillating back and forth.   2. To base or "hinge" upon.

HOLE: inside a hole may indicate the dreamer is "holed up."   2. Financially "in the hole."   3. A shallow hole signifies depression.

HOME: area of origination; where a thought or issue began.

HOMOSEXUALITY: for a heterosexual person, dreaming of homosexuality signifies integrating an aspect of the same polarity as the dreamer.

HORSEMAN: messenger; news.

HOSPITAL: mental, emotional or physical health problem.

HOTEL: a transitory position.

HOUSE: A house symbolizes what the dreamer is "housing." The self and all its aspects.   2. Activities of the mind. An old residence represents old feelings that began when the dreamer lived there; old pattern or theme. One's childhood home indicates a "growth" issue.

  ATTIC: the mind, what the dreamer is "housing upstairs." 2. Old thoughts or ideas that have been stored away.

  BASEMENT: the subconscious.   2. A storage area for repressed or hidden feelings of a lower or coarser nature.

  BATHROOM: a place of elimination. Using the toilet is ridding oneself of something. To wash, shower or bathe is also to eliminate by washing off or cleaning up. A bathroom stall means the dreamer is stalling in getting rid of something.

  BEDROOM: rest or sleep.   2. Sexual activity. See Sleep.

  CEILING: limit; as high as one can go.

  CLOSET: secret or hidden.

  DINING ROOM: an area of assimilation, usually mental.

DOOR: an open door is an opportunity or welcome. Closed means something that is barred to the dreamer.

FLOOR: foundation or support. 2. An issue upon which one takes a stand.

FRAME: framework or plan.

FRONT: the front of the house or front yard is symbolic of conscious activity.

GARDEN: what the dreamer is mentally or spiritually cultivating.

HALLWAY: something the dreamer is passing through to get from one point to another. 2. A connecting passage between two or more related issues. 3. A change or transition.

KITCHEN: a place of preparation; planning or "cooking up" ideas.

LIVING ROOM: an area of activity in the dreamer's life.

REAR: rear entrance and back yard symbolize the subconscious on a general level. Someone sneaking in through the rear means trying to slip something past one's conscious awareness.

THRESHOLD: crossing a threshold is venturing into something. 2. Going inward.

WALLS: to block; keeping something in or out.

WINDOW: the dreamer's point of view. 2. Being shown a "different" viewpoint.

I

ICE: cold feelings; insensitivity.

ICEBERG: much more beneath the surface; partial awareness.

IDIOT: a dumb move; feeling stupid or foolish.

IDOL: a statue-like idol symbolizes one's values.

ILLNESS: mental or physical imbalance. If the dream is precognitive, it will usually depict the influencing conditions such as stress, poor diet, etc.

IMITATION: false; not being genuine or true.

IMPOSTOR: hiding under pretense.

INFANT: new aspect developing.

INFECTION: infectious thoughts or beliefs which are detrimental to the dreamer.

INSECT: insects usually symbolize irritation, what is "bugging" the dreamer.

INTESTINES: affecting the dreamer on a "gut" level.

INTRUDER: intruding thoughts.

IRON: an iron that isn't working, won't heat up or is on a low temperature indicates that the dreamer is low on iron. An overheated iron suggests a hot temperament. Ironing out wrinkles is something the dreamer is attempting to "iron out".

ISLAND: isolated aspect of the dreamer. 2. Solitary, or feelings of isolation.

ITCH: what one is desirous of, or "itching" for.

J

JADE: hardened or jaded feelings.

JAIL: feelings of confinement, restriction.

JAWS: talking too much.

JEANS: if the dreamer dresses for work, jeans signify leisure time or lack of work.   2. Vacation or playtime.

JELLO: inertia; a lifeless mass.

JELLY: fearfulness or cowardice.

JESUS: archetype of love and virtue; the Christ within. 2. Spiritual guidance.

JEWELRY: symbolizes something precious to the dreamer. 2. Valuable advice.

JOB: an issue related to one's employment.

JUDGE: judgmentalness; critical assessment of the self or others.

JUMP: besides excitement, jumping in a dream can signify "taking a leap." Jumping to conclusions. Jumping over (avoiding) something. Advancement by "jumping up."

JUNGLE: the unconscious or subconscious mind.

K

KARATE: skillfully defending oneself.

KERNEL: a seed of truth. 2. The beginning of a viable plan or idea.

KEY: a solution or answer to a problem.

KICK: to assault. 2. Getting a "kick" from something.

KILL: to terminate or end the existence of something.

KINDERGARTEN: learning or beginning something new.

KING: ruling yang (male) aspect.

KISS: to show affection toward, or attraction to someone or something.

KITE: flying "high" or feeling "uplifted."

KITTEN: newly developing aspect, still quite vulnerable.

KNEEL: kneeling before a figure of authority denotes

humbleness, devotion or subservience, depending upon the context of the dream.

KNIFE: to stop or "cut it out." 2. Sharp, cutting words.

KNIGHT: protective quality or trait.

KNOCKING: seeking out or searching for someone or something. 2. An attempt to gain entrance into the dreamer's mind.

KNOT: an entanglement or union with another person. 2. Many knots indicate the dreamers inner feelings of being "tied up in knots."

L

LABEL: importance the dreamer places on things. 2. Labeling others or feeling labeled.

LABORATORY: the "chemistry" in a relationship. 2. Attempting to concoct a "formula for success." 3. Experimentation.

LADDER: the "ladder of success." 2. Advancement or spiritual growth.

LAIR: where one makes their home.

LAMP: an idea or illumination.

LANGUAGE: if it's a foreign language the dreamer doesn't understand, it can mean something the dreamer isn't recognizing. Something foreign or alien to the dreamer. If the dreamer understands what is being said, it means one is disguising their words or not clearly stating their feelings.

LANTERN: guidance is being shown.

LAUNDRY: to divulge or expose; having it "all come out in the wash," or "airing out your dirty laundry." See Wash.

LAWN: outward presentation. Mowing the lawn means manicuring or shaping up one's outer appearance. In one instance, mowing the lawn meant to cut out the "grass" (marijuana).

LEAF: a loose leaf symbolizes aimlessness, while falling leaves reflect the fall season. Sprouting new leaves means a fresh start or new beginning.

LEGS: support, usually concerning values or ideals.

LEMON: something of inferior quality.

LETTER: an informative message.

LIBRARY: seeking or acquiring information.

LIE: lying in a dream indicates being deceived or self-deception.

LIGHT: a bright white light represents enlightenment or spiritual truth. See Ray.

LINE: a boundary or division created by the dreamer.

LIPS: speech. 2. Insincere; "paying lip service."

LIVING ROOM: see House.

LOCOMOTIVE: play on words, crazy or "loco" motive.

LOST: losing an object usually means losing a part of oneself. If one finds oneself lost in a dream it can mean being caught up in something to the exclusion of all else. 2. Losing one's sense of direction in life.

LOUDNESS: loud knocking or speech is an attempt to gain the dreamer's attention.

M

MACHINE: machinery or mechanical parts often portray parts of the body.

MAGAZINE: an issue brought to the attention of the dreamer.

MAILMAN: male-man, a play on words. 2. A message delivered to the dreamer.

MANICURE: man-I-cure, a play on words.

MAP: sometimes a map of inner qualities. 2. Guidance or direction.

MARRIAGE: a partnership or relationship.

MATE: to dream of one's mate usually signifies a highly personalized yin or yang aspect that the dreamer is currently working with. 2. Something to which the dreamer feels "married."

MATTRESS: overly sensitive or a highly sensitive issue.

MEAT: the point or heart of the matter.

MEDICATION: taking medication can mean ingesting something that leaves the dreamer feeling "drugged" or tired. 2. Possible food allergy.

MENSTRUATION: a recurring cycle or period of time. See Blood.

MESS: something in disarray within the dreamer or in the dreamer's life.

MICKEY MOUSE: something of poor quality or workmanship.

MILITARY: strict, discipline.

MILK: life or life-sustaining. 2. Nurturance.

MILKING: Extracting.

MINE: mining is excavating beneath the surface. When one dreams of mining it pertains to something they are extracting from their minds.

MINISTER: what the dreamer is ministering. 2. One's religious or spiritual nature.

MIRROR: reflecting a particular side of the dreamer. 2. One's self-image.

MOANING: to see or hear someone moaning or groaning signifies inner distress.

MONEY: if money is being paid out, it's something "costing" the dreamer, usually non-material items such as health, integrity, etc. Receiving money signifies enrichment.

MOON: a cycle of time. Sometimes precognitive of something that will take place on or about that particular phase.

MOTHER: dominant yin female side. 2. Intuition, guidance or nurturance. 3. What one is "mothering."

MOTHS: old thoughts or feelings.

MOTORCYCLE: one's drive or initiative. 2. Moving quickly.

MOUTH: what the dreamer is verbally expressing.

MOVIE: a presentation of the comedy or drama taking place in the dreamer's life.

MOVING: moving from one residence to another symbolizes something from which the dreamer is either shifting away from or moving toward.

MUSIC: harmonious or inharmonious vibrations, depending upon how the dreamer liked what was being played.

MUSTACHE: outward appearance with which one must face the world.

N

NAIL: caught, the act of getting "nailed." 2. Nailing something means firming or securing, getting it "nailed down."

NARCOTIC: an addiction of the dreamer. See Medication.

NATION: a foreign power indicates a large area involving the dreamer, of which he or she is unaware. The United States pertains to the united aspects of the self, U.S. meaning "us."

NECKLACE: an attractive necklace can symbolize words well-spoken.   2. A cumbersome piece indicates a burden or "millstone."

NECTAR: "sweet talk."   2. To mentally swallow or absorb something pleasant.

NEGLIGEE: partially revealing something of an intimate nature.

NEST: the home.

NEW ZEALAND: finding new enthusiasm or zeal.

NEWSPAPER: informative issue.

NIGHT: something the dreamer is consciously unaware of, or "in the dark" about.

NIGHTFALL: an ending.

NIGHTGOWN: pertaining to late evening activities.

NIPPLE: the nipple of a female's breast symbolizes nurturance, of a bottle: being "weaned."

NOBILITY: noble personages are personifications of noble traits or characteristics of the dreamer.

NOON: a midpoint.

NUDITY: revealing or exposing an aspect of the dreamer. "The naked truth" or "bare facts."

NUMBERS: Numbers are measurements of weight, time or distance. Esoteric levels concerning the significance of numbers are as follows:

ONE: individuality and creativity. The best or the top. A foundation, it is the path of highest expression. In the negative sense, it denotes selfishness with a "me first" attitude. A number assigned to males, beginnings and the self.

TWO: duality, balance and steadfastness. This is the number of the female. It usually means a choice or a pair. In the negative sense it means indecision, vacillation and improper direction.

THREE: intelligence, wisdom and illumination. Expansive or without limitation. Activity or transmutation, it may also signify strength.

FOUR: is the principle of creation as manifested in the four elements: earth, air, fire and water. Dependability, solidarity, practicality and stability.

FIVE: the driving force as expressed in ambition. Movement of all kinds. It is the number of both joy and sorrow and denotes versatility and change. The number of life in physical expression.

SIX: a work number having to do with construction or building. Putting plans or ideas to work. On other levels it can represent a love relationship and sex.

SEVEN: the number of philosophy and science. In dreams it sometimes indicates good fortune or luck.

EIGHT: restriction, discipline, business and financial matters. A number of progression, regeneration and transfiguration. A path toward balance with personal limitations.

NINE: a number of finishing or ending. Letting go of the old for something new. It is also a number of synthesis and sublimation of sexual energies, giving rise to even greater energies. A symbol of transformation, or of death and rebirth.

NUN: play on words for "none."

NURSE: care; the nursing of oneself.

O

OAK: an oak tree is symbolic of strength and longevity. A structure made from oak wood indicates something solid, which will endure.

OCEAN: the depths of oneself. 2. The unconscious. See Water.

OFFICE: the office of one's mind or organizing aspect of oneself.

OLD: an old object that once belonged to the dreamer signifies something from the past, which has in some way been brought to the surface. 2. Old feelings or ideas. 3. That which is redundant or is taking a long time in passing; starting to "get old."

OLDSTERS: older people often personify wiser aspects of the dreamer, although in some cases they may signify the dreamer's feelings about him or herself concerning aging. See Elderly People.

ONION: concerning something that has many layers or levels.

OPTOMETRIST: the need to have one's vision corrected; usually concerning the inner vision.

ORANGE: oranges are a symbol of sunshine and vitality. A dream containing oranges may possibly concern one's health.

ORGASM: a pleasurable ending or climax.

ORIENTAL: play on words: "orienting" oneself. 2. The Orient, being the opposite of Occident. 3. Hidden aspects of the unconscious or subconscious mind.

OUTDOORS: outside the home or home environment.

OVERDRAWN: overdrawn at the bank can signify feeling run-down or depleted of energy.

OVERPASS: crossing a freeway overpass signifies neglecting or passing over an opportunity

OXYGEN: an oxygen tank pertains to one's lungs. To dream of oxygen may indicate health problems.

P

PAINT: painting a house is giving oneself a fresh or new look.   2. Covering up something.

PAIR: two examples of the same thing; usually as seen from different perspectives.

PANTS: leadership or authority role; one who "wears the pants."

PAPER: wrapping paper means to disguise, hide or conceal. Wrapping an object is to finish or "wrap it up."

PARACHUTE: "bailing out" of a situation.

PARK: parking oneself in a particular headspace. The area indicates where one's mind is parked. Parking before entering a store can mean "stopping to think."

PASSENGER: see Automobile.

PAY: paying out money represents something costing the dreamer.

PEANUTS: a small amount; of little value.

PEARLS: pearls are words of wisdom, often signifying spiritual truths.

PENIS: a sensitive, stimulating or private issue.   2. Sexual maturity; manhood. Erect: sexual drive or desire. See Genital Organs.

PHARMACY: related to one's health. See Medication.

PHONE: see Telephone.

PHOTOGRAPH: what the dreamer is "picturing" in his or her mind.

PICKLES: a sorry situation; "in a pickle."

PILLOW: a cushioning effect; "cushioning a blow." 2. Escape through sleep, security.

PIPES: drain or sewage pipes reflect the physical condition of one's body.

PLANE: see Airplane.

PLASTIC: not real; imaginary or imitation.

PLANET: regarding one's plans.

PLAYGROUND: a play area of the mind.

PLUMBER: to dream of a plumber or plumbing fixtures has to do with one's physical condition. See Pipes.

POLICE: watching over or policing oneself. 2. Security.

PRESIDENT: a presiding aspect of the dreamer.

PREGNANT: pregnancy in a dream indicates new developments or ideas that are about to be born.

PSYCHIATRIST: feeling one ought to "have one's head examined."

PURCHASE: to select or elect. 2. Accepting or "buying into."

PURSE: values. See valuables.

R

RADIO: something being broadcast to the dreamer.

RAIN: tears, sadness or depression.

RAKE: to remove or clean up.   2. To "rake in" by profiting. Taken advantage of, as in "raked over the coals."

RAM: see Astrological Signs.

RAPE: a forcible intrusion or entry of an undesirable nature into the dreamer's life.

RAY: a ray of light signifies hope. X-rays are seeing through or beyond. See Light.

RAZOR: a razor blade means division.   2. Cocaine. See Shave.

RECORD: an impression recorded by the dreamer. Listening to a record is playing back what one has mentally recorded. See Music.

REFRIGERATOR: cold feelings which have been stored away.

RELATIVE: something closely related to, or in close association with the dreamer.

RESTAURANT: dining at a restaurant is accepting what is being served or "dished out."   2. Dietary.

RING: a relationship. Wedding rings symbolize a marriage relationship. To lose one's ring means something in the relationship is lost or missing.

RIVER: course or direction; the flow of one's life.

ROAD: a direction the dreamer is taking. A crossroad indicates a major decision that may affect the dreamer's life.

ROCK: obstacles such as "a rocky road."   2. Something solid.

ROOF: that which is covering the dreamer's mind.

ROLLER COASTER: emotional ups and downs.

ROLLER SKATES: very active or busy.

ROOM: indicates a space the dreamer has reserved within, usually housing a particular set of feelings.

ROOTS: a sense of belonging or feeling at home. 2. Deep or firmly entrenched feelings.

ROSE: roses are symbols of love and affection. A white rose denotes purity, pink: affection and red: love.

ROUTE: a direction one is taking. 2. Routine activities.

RULER: something the dreamer is measuring or comparing.

RUNNING: haste. 2. Something the dreamer is running toward or away from.

S

SCALES: what is weighing or being weighed in one's mind. Bathroom scales usually indicate the dreamer's concern about weight or dieting. See Astrological Signs.

SCHOOL: the school of life; what the dreamer is learning or being "schooled" in. High school usually represents higher knowledge or sound advice.

SCORPION: see Astrological Signs.

SEW: to mend (as in a relationship). 2. To close up by bringing together, like in a merger or business transaction.

SEX: sexual intercourse primarily means union or integration. An intercourse is always an exchange. In the common vernacular it has many meanings. An unpleasant exchange could mean "getting screwed" or "getting reamed." "Screwing up" is another common expression. I am sure the reader can think of additional symbology. See section on sexual dreams.

SHAFT: getting "shafted." The dreamer who contributed this interpretation dreamt of falling down an elevator shaft.

SHAMPOO: shampooing of the hair means cleaning up one's thoughts.

SHARKS: unscrupulous or predatory individuals.

SHAVE: removing unwanted growth. To cut oneself while shaving signifies defacement.

SHELF: to "shelve" or set aside.

SHIP: the voyage of life; a "course" one has mapped out or charted for themselves. See Boat.

SHOES: a role or activity. Sandals: spirituality, loafers: inactivity, black high heels: romance and sex, dress shoes: business, sneakers: leisure.

SHOOT: being shot at or shooting a gun is symbolic of a verbal assault; being "shot down." See Gun.

SHOPPING: seeking or making a selection; what the dreamer is "shopping" for.

SIDEWALK: a side issue of the major theme of the dream.

SIGN: a direction. 2. Indication as to where the dreamer is at on some level.

SKIING: snow skiing can mean "skimming the surface." Water skiing is being influenced or "towed" along by a particular idea or individual, usually the driver of the boat.

SKIN: sensitivity. 2. Superficial, as in "skin-deep."

SLACKS: a lessening or "slacking."

SLEEPING: to dream of someone asleep signifies being unconscious or unaware of what is going on; "asleep at the switch."

SLIDE: going down a slide or sliding down something means worsening. If the dreamer is playing and having fun in the dream, it may indicate the dreamer is oblivious to what is happening.

SOLDIER: preparing for combat, usually an illness.

SPACECRAFT: often a literal astral encounter. A spiritual or mystical experience.

SPIDER: a venomous female. 2. A spider working on a web represents plans that are being made.

SPIGOT: see faucet.

SPONGE: what the dreamer is absorbing.

SPY: a spy, whether a secret agent or merely someone looking through a peephole indicates the dreamer is viewing something covertly.

STAB: to injure with words. 2. To injure underhandedly, as in "stabbed in the back."

STEPS or STAIRS: measures or "steps" that are being taken. 2. Degree of advancement.

STOPPED: something preventing passage of the dreamer. A traffic light, stalled vehicle, etc., will determine whether the dream is saying "stop and look," or stalled and stuck. It may be a message to quit, slow down or even to reflect.

STORE: where one's thoughts and feelings are stored. A grocery store can signify dietary selection.

STORM: emotional turmoil.

STOVE: to implement or plan; an instrument for "cooking up" ideas.

STREAM: the "stream" of time.

STREET: an "avenue," option or direction.

STRING: attachment. 2. To be led as in "stringing along."

STUDIO: a "studious" environment.

SUBWAY: subconscious transportation.

SUITE: indulging in sweets.

SUNRISE: a new beginning. 2. Something that's "arising" or "coming up."

SWIMMING: thoughts or feelings the dreamer is immersed in.

SWIMMING POOL: the pool of the mind.

SWORD: courage or truth.

T

TAB: a bar or dinner tab usually means keeping "tabs" on one's diet or indulgences.

TABLE: to temporarily set aside. Sitting at a table with a friend or friends signifies a good relationship. Alone at a table can mean emptiness or solitude in one's life.

TEETH: words. False teeth are lies, gold teeth: words of wisdom, loose: loose talk, falling out: talking too much, braces: controlled speech, sharp or pointed teeth: "sharp" or "pointed" words.

TELEPHONE: communication or contact with another. 2. Communicating with a particular aspect of oneself.

TELEVISION: a "telling vision," usually of the dreamer.

TEMPERATURE: an indication of one's feelings or emotional condition.

TERMITES: what is eating away at the dreamer, often attacking the foundation of one's thoughts or premises.

THEATER: sitting in a theater is witnessing a dramatic event in the life of the dreamer. 2. The "projection" of one's thoughts or feelings.

THIEF: to rob or cheat oneself of something, quite often related to health.

TIDE: a cycle of time. Ebb or low tide means a lessening, that which has run out in the dreamer's life. Outgoing tide is diminishing while incoming tide is replenishing or increasing.

TIGHTS: wearing tights symbolizes a "tight" situation, possibly a financial squeeze.

TIP: leaving money as a tip signifies receiving good advice.

TIRE: an automobile tire represents the energy one "rides" on.

TOILET: a place to eliminate. Using the toilet means "getting rid" of something undesirable. See Bathroom.

TOMB: abode of the enlightened or illumined self.

TOOLS: capabilities.   2. Repairing, or something in need of repair.

TOOTH: truth; a cavity or hole in one's tooth means not telling the whole truth.

TOOTHBRUSH: brushing one's teeth indicates brushing up on one's vocabulary or verbal presentation.

TONGUE: related to positive or negative speech as shown in the dream.   2. Gossip.

TOYS: what the dreamer is playing or "toying" with.

TRAILER: what is trailing behind the dreamer. In this instance it was trailing health.

TRAIN: a train of thought.   2. "A one-track mind." A fast-moving train indicates rushing. A freight train: laden or burdened. A train without or off the tracks means the dreamer is "off the track."

TREASURE: discovering buried treasure is unearthing riches of the mind or hidden talents.

TREE: growth or development. Fruit trees represent productivity; what the dreamer is producing or has produced.

TRUCK: see Automobile.

TUBING: relating to the physical body or health of the dreamer.

TWILIGHT: dim awareness.

TWINS: duality. Both sides of an issue; pro and con. See Astrological Signs.

U

UMBRELLA: to shield or protect oneself, usually from emotion.

UMPIRE: a decision-making aspect of the dreamer.

UNDERGROUND: the deeper or subconscious levels of the mind.

UNDERWEAR: inner or personal feelings.

UNDRESS: to expose or reveal one's feelings.

UNIFORM: a role of the dreamer. Military is discipline, police: what the dreamer is policing, etc.

UNITED STATES: see Nation.

URINATE: eliminating or letting go of something of a yin nature. See Toilet.

UTENSIL: look for play on words with eating utensils, such as "spooning it up," "forking it over," "cutting up," etc.

V

VACANT: a vacant room or dwelling can indicate lack of thought or not using one's mind in a given area.

VACATION: sometimes insinuating the dreamer's mind is on vacation.   2. An indication that the dreamer needs to take a break.

VACCINATE: immunizing oneself from others whom the dreamer finds offensive.

VACUUM CLEANER: detachment or insensitivity.   2. One's feelings are swept up in a vacuum.

VAGINA: a private or sexual matter. See Genital Organs.

VAGUENESS: sometimes a vague dream or vagueness in a dream represents something the dreamer is only vaguely aware of.

VALLEY: a place of security.

VALUABLES: inner values; morals, ethics, etc.

VALVE: a malfunctioning valve may indicate health problems. See Faucet.

VAMPIRE: personification of something or someone the dreamer finds energy-draining.

VASE: the human vessel or receptacle of our contents.

VINEYARD: production of one's spiritual efforts. The quality of the grapes represents the dreamer's inner qualities.

VIRGIN: new, innocent or inexperienced. See Astrological Signs.

VOLCANO: an angry eruption, inner turmoil.

W

WADING: wading in the water is "getting one's feet wet," wading into a new situation.

WAITER OR WAITRESS: concerns what the dreamer is "waiting" for, or what "awaits one."

WALL: a barrier or enclosure; what the dreamer is attempting to keep in or out.

WALLET: one's identity; what the dreamer is identifying with.

WAR: conflict within oneself. 2. Battling an illness.

WAREHOUSE: what one is storing or has stored away in their minds.

WASH: washing clothes is "cleaning up one's act." Freshly washed or laundered clothes is putting on a "fresh appearance." 2. The truth; having it "all come out in the wash." See laundry.

WATER: mental and emotional conditions. Rough water indicates hard times while smooth water means the reverse. Clear water symbolizes clear perception, murky water, unclear thoughts. See Astrological Signs.

WAVES: emotions; difficult to overwhelming conditions, depending upon the height of the waves.

WAX: something made out of wax symbolizes a temporary or impermanent situation.

WEATHER: attitude, disposition or emotional climate.

WEB: plans or ideas that the dreamer has either spun or is caught up in. See Spider.

WEEDS: destructive or counterproductive thoughts. What the dreamer needs to "weed out."

WEIGHT: if a weight is indicated in numbers it may mean a passage of time, otherwise it signifies an amount. Carrying something heavy is to be burdened or "weighed down."

WELL: inner or subconscious knowledge being brought to the surface.

WHIP: to dream of whipping someone or something signifies that which the dreamer is "whipping into shape."

WIG: misleading or deceptive thoughts.

WINDY: long windedness.

WINDOW: see House.

WINE: in "good spirits." 2. Friendship or camaraderie; a cause to celebrate.

WITCH: negative female or feminine attribute.

WOOD: a wooden stump or block can indicate hard headedness.

✐Notes

Chapter I

1. Woodward, Mary Ann, *Edgar Cayce's Story of Karma* (New York: Berkley Publishing Corporation, 1971), p. 13

2. Fagan, Joen and Shepard, Irma Lee, *Gestalt Therapy Now* (New York: Harper & Row, 1970), p. 27

3. Dement, William C., *Some Must Watch While Some Must Sleep* (New York: W. W. Norton & Co., 1972), p. 22

4. Jung, C. G., *Dreams* (New Jersey: Princeton University Press, 1974), p. 101

Chapter 2

1. *Holy Bible, The,* King James Version (New York: World Publishing Company, 1978) p. 16.

2. Mahoney, Maria F., *The Meaning in Dreams and Dreaming* (New Jersey: The Citadel Press, 1966), p. 48.

3. Ibid., p. 54

4. Bailey, Alice A., *Esoteric Psychology, Volume II* (New York: Lucis Publishing Company, 1970), p. 505.

5. Furst, Jeffery, *Edgar Cayce's Story of Attitudes and*

Emotions (New York: Berkley Publishing Corporation, 1976), p. 15.

6.   Perls, Frederick, *Gestalt Therapy Verbatim* (Utah: Real People Press, 1981), p. 19.

7.   Faraday, Ann, *The Dream Game* (New York: Harper & Row, 1974), p. 170.

Chapter 3

1.   Blofeld, John, *The Tantric Mysticism of Tibet* (New York: Causeway Books, 1974), p. 221.

Chapter 4

1.   Hall, Calvin, *The Meaning of Dreams* (New York: McGraw-Hill Book Company, 1966), p. 16.

2.   Faraday, Ann, *The Dream Game* (New York: Harper & Row, 1974), p. 235.

3.   Ibid. p. 234.

4.   McGarey, William A., *The Edgar Cayce Remedies* (New York: Bantam Books, Inc., 1983), p. 13.

5.   Furst, Jeffery, *Edgar Cayce's Story of Attitudes and Emotions* (New York: Berkley Publishing Corporation, 1976), p. 31.

6.   Holmes, Ernest, *The Science of Mind* (New York: Dodd, Mead and Company, 1938), p. 234.

7.   Freud, Sigmund, *The Interpretation of Dreams* (New York: Avon Books, 1965), p. 588.

8.   Ullman, Montague and Zimmerman, Nan, *Working With Dreams* (New York: Dell Publishing Co., Inc., 1979), p. 45.

9.   Tart, Charles, *Altered States of Consciousness* (New York:

Doubleday, 1972), p. 164.

10. Garfield, Patricia, *Creative Dreaming* (New York: Ballantine Books, 1976), p. 84.

11. Ibid. p. 127.

12. Ibid. p. 21

Chapter 5

1. Windsor, Joan, *The Inner Eye* (New York: Berkley Publishing Group, 1991), p. 13.

2. Bayliss, Janice, *Dream Dynamics and Decoding: an Interpretation Manual* (California: Sun, Man, Moon, Inc., 1976), p. 1.

3. Heindel, Max, *Occult Principles of Health and Healing* (California: Rosicrucian Fellowship, 1938), p. 51.

Chapter 6

1. Delaney, Gayle, *Living Your Dreams* (New York: Harper & Row, 1981), pp. 7-11, 21-28.

Chapter 7

1. Jung, Carl G., *Man and His Symbols* (New York: Dell Publishing Co. 1979), p. 169.

2. Maslow, Abraham H. *The Farther Reaches of Human Nature* (New York: Viking Press, 1971), p. 299

3. Assagioli, Roberto, *Psychosynthesis,* (New York: Viking Press, 1971), p. 38.

4. Rama, Swami, with Ballentine, Rudolph & Ajaya, Swami, *Yoga and Psychotherapy* (Pennsylvania: Himalayan International Institute, 1976), p. 248.

Bibliography

Bailey, Alice A. *Esoteric Psychology, Vols. I & II*. New York: Lucis Publishing Co., 1970.

Bayliss, Janice. *Dream Dynamics and Decoding: an Interpretation Manual*. Huntington Beach, CA: Sun, Man, Moon Inc., 1976.

Blofeld, John. *The Tantric Mysticism of Tibet*. New York: Causeway Books, 1974.

Bro, Harmon. *Edgar Cayce on Dreams*. New York: Warner Books, 1968.

Bucke, Richard. *Cosmic Consciousness*. New York: University Books, 1961.

Castenada, Carlos. *The Teachings of Don Juan: A Yaqui Way of Knowledge*. New York: Ballantine Books, Inc., 1969.

Cayce, Edgar. Compiled by Marilyn Lingren Peterson. *Dreams and Dreaming, Parts I & II*. Virginia Beach, VA: A.R.E, Inc. 1976

Cooper, J. C. *Symbolism: The Universal Language.* Wellingborough, Northamptonshire, England: The Aquarian Press, 1982.

Delaney, Gayle. *Living Your Dreams.* New York: Harper & Row, 1979.

Dement, William C. *Some Must Watch While Others Must Sleep.* New York: W. W. Norton & Co., Inc. 1972.

Denning, Melita and Phillips, Osborne. *The Llewellyn Practical Guide to Astral Projection.* St. Paul: Llewellyn Publications, 1979.

Faraday, Ann. *Dream Power.* New York: Berkley Books, 1973.

Faraday, Ann. *The Dream Game.* New York: Harper & Row, 1974.

Fiore, Edith. *You Have Been Here Before.* New York: Ballantine Books. 1979.

Freud, Sigmund. *The Interpretation of Dreams.* New York: Avon Books, 1965.

Fromm, Erich. *The Forgotten Language.* New York: Grove Press, Inc., 1978.

Furst, Jeffery. *Edgar Cayce's Story of Attitudes and Emotions.* New York: Berkley Publishing Corp., 1972.

Garfield, Patricia. *Creative Dreaming.* New York: Ballantine Books, 1976.

Hall, Calvin S. *The Meaning of Dreams.* New York: McGraw-

Hill Book Company, 1966.

Head, Joseph and Cranston, S. L. *Reincarnation, an East-West Anthology.* Wheaton, IL: The Theosophical Publishing House, 1981.

Heline, Corrine. *Healing and Regeneration through Color.* Santa Barbara, CA: J. F. Rowny Press, 1972.

Heline, Corrine. *Sacred Science of Numbers.* Los Angeles, CA: New Age press, Inc., 1977.

Holmes, Ernest. *The Science of Mind.* New York: Dodd, Mead and Company, 1938.

Jung, C. G. *Dreams.* New Jersey: Princeton University Press, 1974.

Jung, Carl G. *Man and His Symbols.* New York: Dell Publishing Co. Inc., 1979.

Jung, C. G. *Memories, Dreams and Reflections.* New York: Vintage Books, 1965.

Keltzer, Kenneth. *The Sun and the Shadow.* Virginia Beach, VA: A.R.E. Press. 1987.

Keyes, Ken. Jr. *Handbook to Higher Consciousness.* Coos Bay, OR: Living Love Publications, 1984.

LaBerge, Stephen. *Lucid Dreaming.* Los Angeles, CA: Jeremy P. Tarcher, Inc., 1985.

Langley, Noel. *Edgar Cayce on Reincarnation.* New York: Warner Books, Inc., 1973.

Leadbeater, C.W. *Man Visible and Invisible.* Wheaton, IL: The Theosophical Publishing House, 1972.

Leadbeater, C. W. *The Chakras.* Wheaton, IL: The Theosophical Publishing House, 1927.

Mahoney, Maria. *The Meaning in Dreams and Dreaming.* New Jersey: The Citadel Press, 1966.

McGarey, William A. *The Edgar Cayce Remedies.* New York: Bantam Books, Inc., 1983.

Monroe, Robert A. *Journeys Out of the Body.* New York: Doubleday & Company, Inc., 1971.

Moody, Raymond A. *Life After Life.* New York: Bantam Books, Inc., 1976.

Perls, Frederick S. *Gestalt Therapy Verbatim.* New York: Bantam Books, Inc,. 1971.

Perkins, James S. *Experiencing Reincarnation.* Wheaton, IL: The Theosophical Publishing House, 1977.

Rama, Swami, with Ballentine, Rudolph, and Ajaya, Swami. *Yoga and Psychotherapy: The Evolution of Consciousness.* Honesdale, PA: The Himalayan Institute of Yoga Science and Philosophy, 1976.

Reed, Henry. *Edgar Cayce on Mysteries of the Mind.* New York: Warner Books, Inc., 1989.

Roberts, Jane. *Seth Speaks.* New York: Bantam Books, Inc., 1972.

Rogo, D. Scott. *Leaving the Body.* New Jersey: Prentice-Hall, Inc., 1983.

Rutter, Owen. *The Scales of Karma.* New York: Samuel Weiser, Inc., 1971.

Schucman, Helen, and Thetford, William. *A Course in Miracles.* Tiburon, CA.: Foundation for Inner Peace, 1976.

Sannella, Lee. *Kundalini-Psychosis or Transcendence?* San Francisco, CA: H.S. Dakin Company, 1976.

Sechrist, Elsie. *Dreams: Your Magic Mirror.* New York: Warner Books, 1968.

Sharma, I.C. *Cayce, Karma and Reincarnation.* New York: Harper & Row, 1975.

Smith, Roy C. *Incarnation and Reincarnation.* Los Angeles, CA: Religious Research Press, 1975.

Sparrow, G. Scott. *Lucid Dreaming: Dawning of the Clear Light.* Virginia Beach, VA: A.R.E. Press, 1982.

Sparrow, Lynn Elwell. *Reincarnation: Claiming your Past, Creating Your Future.* New York: Harper & Row, 1988.

Sutphen, Dick, and Taylor, Lauren Leigh. *Past-Life Therapy in Action.* Malibu, CA: Valley of the Sun Publishing Co., 1983.

Tart, Charles. *Altered States of Consciousness.* New York: Doubleday & Co., 1969.

Taylor, A. E. *Elements of Metaphysics.* New York: Barnes & Noble, Inc. 1961.

Thurston, Mark. *How to Interpret Your Dreams.* Virginia Beach, VA: A.R.E Press, 1978.

Ullman, Montague, and Zimmerman, Nan. *Working With Dreams.* New York: Dell Publishing Co., 1980.

Wambach, Helen. *Life Before Life.* New York: Bantam Books, Inc., 1979.

Windsor, Joan. *The Inner Eye: Your Dreams Can Make You Psychic.* New Jersey: Prentice-Hall, Inc., 1985.

Woodward, Mary Ann. *Edgar Cayce's Story of Karma.* New York: Berkley Publishing Corp., 1972

Index